How To Talk So Kids Will Listen & Love Languages of Kids

Practical Survival Guide To Parenting With Love And Logic

By HealthMedicine Press

Legal Disclaimer:

Please note that the information in this book is for educational and informational purposes only. The purpose of this book is to provide information with currently available knowledge and understanding based on the author's best efforts at that time without any kind, express, or implied warranty. It is NOT intended to be used as a substitute for any advice (including but not limited to) Legal, Technology, Business, and Medical: advice, diagnosis, treatment, or any other services.

Readers should use their judgment and own advisors for all decisions and should not base or rely on this book for any decisions. We disclaim all warranties or implied warranties concerning all content on this book. Readers should consult their health providers or/and national/local health authorities for any treatment or preventive guidelines. Readers should consult their business professionals for any business advice. Readers should consult an attorney for any legal advice.

The author(s) have made every effort to provide accurate, reliable, and up-to-date information, while due to the possibility of human errors or change/updates, author(s) do not guarantee that all information included is complete or accurate, and disclaim all responsibilities for any omissions or error, or the results obtained from using the information contained in this document.

Any contents regarding any trends on what the author(s) believe regarding jobs, industries, technology, or other topics, etc., are all based on the authors' opinion. As we all know, no one can predict the future. There is no express or implied warranty that any of these opinions will happen in the future.

We have no obligation to warrant the accuracy or appropriateness of any third-party websites or URLs. The listing of any person, business, hyperlinks, or others in this book does not constitute an endorsement or recommendation by the author(s). The author(s) are not responsible for the opinions or comments of others the author(s) use as quotes. The author(s) do not warrant, endorse, guarantee, or assume responsibility for any information offered in the articles and hyperlinks of third-party authors referenced in the book. If a reader chooses to click on links and be taken to an external website belonging to a third party, then the reader and only the reader shall be responsible and liable for his/her actions should you suffer or incur any harm or loss from the usage of such information

Certain characters, stories, and data are used for illustration purposes to help explain certain concepts in the book. There are no explicit or implied warranties that these are (including but not limited to) actual people, events, stories, data, etc.

By reading this, the reader agrees that under no circumstances is the author(s) responsible for any direct or indirect losses incurred due to using this document's information, including not limited to omissions, inaccuracies, or errors. You agree to hold the author(s) harmless from ALL (including but not limited to) claims, losses, damages, etc.

Table of Contents

Introduction..1

Section 1:..5

Prepare Your Kids For Better Communication..5

1. Helping kids Manage Emotions 5

2. Engaging Cooperation........................... 22

3. Encouraging Autonomy 32

Section 2:..43

Get Your Kids to Listen..43

1. Empowering Ways To Get Kids To Listen 43

2. How to Get Your Kids to Listen the First Time You Speak.. 48

3. Correcting Behaviors In Kids Who Won't Listen.. 54

Section 3:..63

How To Talk to Kids..63

1. How To Talk To Kids 63

2. How to Talk to Kids about Difficult Topics 67

3. How to Talk to Kids about Sexual Harassment.. 77

4. How to Talk to Kids about the Divorce... 80

5. It's Never Too Early To Talk To Kids About Social Media Habits 93

6. How to Talk To Kids About Bullying 97

7. Proven Strategies to Finally Stop Yelling 106

Section 4: 114

Get Your Kids To Talk To You 114

– Age-By-Age Guide 114

Section 5: 122

How To Resolve Conflicts Effectively 122

1. Parent-Child Conflicts 122

2. Friendship Conflicts 140

Section 6: 145

Love Languages of Kids 145

1. What Are the Love Languages Of Kids 145

2. How To Connect Your Kids Using Love Languages 154

Conclusion 169

From the Author 172

References 173

Introduction

A new study has reported that more than 70% of parents say they "struggle" to communicate with their kids meaningfully. Communicating with your kids should be easy, but miscommunication is easier.

You asked them what they had for lunch, and they assumed it's an attack about their diet. You just made a simple comment about what they are wearing, and they storm off and slam the door. You and your kid seem to argue continually, and you wish you could have a parent translator. Or you were just trying to show how much you cared about them, but their reactions suggest you are speaking a different language.

On the other hand, talking with your kids is a daily event. However, let's face it, as parents, we are busy. It is easier for us to keep the conversation with our kids light so that we can move on to the next thing on our "to-do" list, even though our kids do need you to tune in and listen more deeply.

All these situations need to be changed immediately.

Kids base their views of themselves as well as the whole world on their daily experiences. As parents, one of the most critical experiences you can provide for your kids is to talk and listen to them. Kids and adults can develop positive relationships through these daily interactions, which will help kids learn about themselves and the world positively and effectively.

You will find parenting can be more enjoyable once the positive parent-children relationship is established by talking and communicating with your kids in a proper way. Whether you are parenting a toddler or a teenager, healthy communication is the key to build kids' self-esteem and mutual respect. The way you talk to your kids teaches them how to talk to others as well.

The **How To Talk So Kids Will Listen & Love Languages of Kids** covers the most updated approaches and techniques you will want to know about how to communicate with your kids effectively and appropriately.

You will learn:

- **Prepare Your Kids For Better Communication:**
  - Helping kids manage emotions, engaging cooperations & encouraging autonomy;
- **Get Your Kids To Listen**
  - How to get your kids to listen the first time you speak;
  - What to do if your kids don't listen;
- **How To Talk To Kids**
  - What are the ways to talk to kids that will work;
  - How to talk about difficult topics, sexual harassment, divorce, social media habits & bullying;
  - Proven strategies to finally stop yelling at your kids;
- **How To Get Your Kids Talk To You (Age-by-Age Guide)**
- **How To Resolve Conflicts Effectively** (Both Parent-Child Conflicts & Friendship Conflicts)
- **Love Languages of Kids**
  - What are the love languages of Kids;
  - How to connect your kids using love languages;

Building an open, trustful, and loving relationship with their kids is the dream of almost every parent. One of the most practical and mutually rewarding ways to achieve this is by appropriate and positive communication. This book is not just a theoretical presentation. You will learn practical, tried-and-true, and science-based parenting communication approaches with specific examples.

Let' nail parent-child communication together. You love your kids, as I do mine, so I know you will try.

Thank you for purchasing this book!

You can get a 30-page Help Guide: **Listening Activities For Kids** & updates on this book for FREE by sending an email to **HealthMedicineMDMPH@gmail.com** with the book name in the subject line.

You May Also Like:

Coronavirus & COVID-19 Pandemic: Past, Present, Future: 2 Books In 1: Learn How To Protect Yourself And Your Loved Ones & What Post Pandemic Opportunities Are

Section 1

Prepare Your Kids For Better Communication

1. Helping kids Manage Emotions

Feelings can be complex, especially for a 4-year-old who does not understand why you didn't allow them to have another cookie or a 7-year-old who gets upset that you got called from work and had to leave the playground early. Helping kids cope with their feelings is tricky, while this is an essential part of parenting.

1.1 Why Emotional Understand is Crucial for Your Kid

One certainty of parenting is that your kid will regularly face circumstances he/she doesn't like and experience all kinds of emotions (can even be all in one day sometimes!). Teaching your kids how to identify their emotions as well as express and handle those emotions appropriately will help them become mentally strong, leading happier and more fulfilling lives. The kids who can understand their feelings and have the skills to cope with them will be confident that they will be able to handle whatever lives throw in their ways.

Developing emotional skills will help your kids develop empathy, relate better to others, manage their own behaviors, and deal with all types of situations. It will also be greatly beneficial to your parent-child relationship since your kids will grow in their capacities to explain their frustrations or disappointments with words instead of acting out. A child saying: "I'm mad at you!" is less likely to hit. And a kid who said: "That really hurts my feelings" is better equipped to peacefully resolve the conflict.

We will not be able to insulate our kids from the ups and downs of life as parents. What we can do is teach our kids how to navigate these experiences in a way that preserves and enhances their life relationships as well as grow their personal characters.

1.2 Understanding Your Kid's feelings

Kids deal with the same complex and uncomfortable emotions as adults-disappointment, frustration, anger, worry, embarrassment, sadness, etc. However, unlike us, young kids usually don't have the words and skills to express how they're feeling and face those emotions.

Instead, kids often express their emotions in other ways. They communicate through their play or behavior; sometimes, they act out their emotions in inappropriate, physical, or problematic approaches.

As early as your children were born, they already began to learn the emotional skills: identifying, expressing, and managing their emotions. They learned these skills through their social interactions and close relationships with the important people in their lives, including parents and grandparents.

Being the parent means you have a vital role in assisting your kids in understanding their emotions and behaviors. It would be best to show them how to manage their emotions constructively and positively.

1.3 Step-by-Step to Raise Emotionally Intelligent Kids

1. **Be Aware of Emotions**

Being a parent can be stressful and non-stop. It's often not like running the marathon; instead, it's like running till death. We naturally tend to look around as things finally get calm and think, "There's nothing currently on fire. Nice, life is good. "But this is like standing in the coal mine and ignoring tons of dead canaries. Emotions usually precede outbursts. So it's critical noticing the kids' emotions at the early stage.

"Not misbehaving" is not equal to "not upset." For example, when the spouse crosses his/her arms and says scowlingly, "I'm fine," you know he/she is not fine at all and behaves in a passive-aggressive way. For kids, they may not even understand their feelings and how to express them appropritately. So noticing and being aware of their feelings early can prevent unwanted behaviors.

However, many parents cannot notice their own feelings. Studies have shown that to feel what their children are feeling as parents, they must be aware of feelings, first in themselves and then in their children. If you cannot be aware of your own feelings, you will have difficulty relating to others' feelings, including your children's.

Emotional awareness refers to recognizing and identifying your emotions, and being sensitive to the presence of other people's feelings. You don't need to afraid of showing your feelings in front of your kids. Even anger has its place as long as it's expressed constructively and respectfully. If you hold back from showing emotions, then your kids will learn, "Dad and Mom don't have these emotions, neither should I."

Kids need a role model for feelings too. Seeing arguments and then seeing how they're resolved constructively is far better and helpful than never seeing them. Ironically, some "super-parents" who tried to hide their feelings find out that their kids will be less capable of coping with negative emotions than they would have been if they have shown their own emotions in a reasonable way. This is because their kids have grown up emotionally distant from them and the kids lacked a role model to teach them how to deal with the difficult feelings effectively.

Noticing emotions now and avoid the crisis later. Shielding children from difficult emotional situations and then sending them into the outside world is like sending the athletes to the Olympics without training.

2. Help Kids Recognize Their Emotions

- **Teach Kids About Emotions**

The first step in handling emotions is knowing what they are. Explain that everyone has emotions, and some are feeling good, but others may not. More importantly, let them know that sharing feelings is totally okay, including the uncomfortable ones.

Teach kids feelings by naming the feelings for them. For example, you can say, "I can tell you are sad" or "You look happy right now." You also can express more specifically, "I'm angry because those boys were mean today" or "I am sad that we cannot go camping tomorrow."

Ask your kids to name all the emotional words they can think of and write them down. Discuss and talk about how each one feels. Simultaneously, emphasizing that all emotions are considered friendly messengers that not permanent, and they just come and go. You can also post this list somewhere visible and grow this list when new feelings arise.

Another effective way is striking up conversions about emotions by discussing how various characters on TV or in books. Every once in a while, pause and ask, "How do you think this character is feeling now?" Then, talk about the different emotions the character may experiences and explain why. With practice, your kids will improve their abilities to label their feelings.

- **Talk about Emotions**

After the kids know what the emotions are, show them how to use those emotional words daily. Be a role model to express feelings by sharing your feelings. For example, say, "I feel sad that you didn't want to share your cookies with your brother today. I bet he is feeling sad too."

Every day, ask your kid, "How are you feeling today?". For young children, it may be helpful to use a simple chart with smiley faces, let them choose one, and talk about it.

Also, point out when noticing your kid may be having a particular emotion. For example, say, "You look upset when we cannot visit grandma today." Or "It looks like you are happy playing at the park."

- **Explain Emotions and Behaviors**

Learning how to express feelings in a socially appropriate way is also critical. They also need to know that throwing a temper tantrum at school or screaming in the middle of the supermarket is not okay. So if they feel upset, it doesn't mean they can just roll around on the floor crying as it disrupts others. It's not acceptable to hit even though they feel angry.

What they need to learn is disciplining their behaviors, not their feelings. Say, "You are losing the toy for the rest of the day because you are screaming, and it bothers other people." Or "You are going to time-out because you just hit your brother. "

3. Identify What Has Triggered Their Feelings

After kids understand what emotions are, it's time to figure out where they come from. Help your kids by explaining to them that the emotions are often caused by something that happened around us.

As your kid comes to you feeling upset, talk about what just happened before the feeling arose. Being their parents, we are able to dig deeper to assist in identifying what's the trigger for that new emotion. When your kid reaches out to you, you need to understand that your kid is the height of his/her emotional response, which means the brain's emotional center is active and doesn't have the capacity for rational thinking nor language. So it's not a good time for a long conversion. Instead, using simple questions and words to find out what just happened.

4. Listen Empathetically And Validate Their Emotions

Most of the time, emotions are not logical. You won't expect a kid to understand how to manage negative emotions. Let's admit that we can still have problems handling those feelings even after decades of experience as adults.

Use empathetic listening to help your kids clarify and get them to talk. They can notice whether you are frustrated or impatient. They will need to feel you can understand them and are their sides. Listening is far more than using your ears to collect the data. Empathetic listeners will watch for the physical evidence of their kids' feelings and try to see the situation from the kids' perspectives. Their words are said out in a noncritical and soothing way to reflect on what they have heard.

It's also important to accept all feelings, but not necessarily all behaviors. Sometimes parents will inadvertently minimize their kids' emotions and send out the wrong messages. Saying, "It's not a big deal, just stop being so upset." will make your kid think their emotions are wrong. However, even if you consider them out of proportion, these emotions are okay. Understandably, parents tend to jump right in and solve the problems directly when the kids are experiencing big negative feelings. But this will miss a vital step.

Before we move into the problem-solving stage, take a moment to validate your kids' feelings. Whether you think they are frustrated, sad, mad, or disappointed, put a name to their feeling. Then, be empathetic and demonstrate that you understand how they are feeling. For example, say, “I know you get upset as we cannot go to the beach today. I will also get frustrated when I don’t get things going as I want to.” This extra element can reinforce to your kid that their feelings are really understood.

Validation allows kids to know their emotions make sense. If parents try to fix the issue immediately by saying, “Stop crying! It’s not that bad!”, kids will learn some emotions are not acceptable and will be safer not to experience their feelings. In this case, kids are losing the opportunity to learn from the difficult experiences and understand all emotions are valid, just some feelings are “good” and some are “bad”.

Simultaneously, helping kids understand what they are feeling right now will not last forever, and the emotions come and go. This can help the kid stay calmer in the middle of a big emotional moment.

Sometimes, it’s struggling for parents to know how to respond to overly emotional children, but please remind yourself that it does not mean your child is weak by being emotional. It’s normal for kids to have intense emotions. In fact, knowing how to identify and handle these emotions will make them mentally stronger.

Some parents may complain their kids are too sensitive and assume that their sensitivity can be fixed. While sensitivity is part of your kid's natural temperament since everyone has a different one. Be sure your kid knows that you are fine with this and accept them for who they are.

5. Setting Limits & Teaching Coping Strategies

Just because the kids feel intense emotions, does not mean they need to allow their emotions to control them. Again, all emotions are acceptable; however, all behaviors are not. You need to set limits.

After parents acknowledged the feeling behind those misbehaviors, validated and help kids label them, parents can make sure kids understand certain behaviors cannot be tolerated or inappropriate. Then parents could guide the kid into thinking of other appropriate ways to manage negative emotions. "You're angry that your brother took that toy away from you," the parents could say. "I would feel the same, too. But it is not okay for you to hit your brother. What else can you do instead?"

After you have listened empathetically, validated or labeled their feelings, and set limits on the misbehaviors, now it's time to fix issues. Here are some useful skills to teach kids how to handle their emotions appropriately.

- **Counting to calm down**. Teach your kids to distract themselves from negative thoughts by counting. Counting sheep or ceiling tiles to 10 or counting down from 100 are examples of the mental tasks that can help reduce their distress.
- **Practicing deep breathing**. Teach kids how to breathe in a slow and quiet way through their noses and then out their mouths. Repeat several times until they have calmed down.
- **Taking a break**. Allow children to give themselves a brief time-out to collect themselves. It can be going to get the water or a drink or stepping into another room for minutes. Then, they are in control of deciding when they're reading to come out.
- **Preparing the calm-down kit**. You can fill a box with some items that can help your children cheer up or calm down—for example, pictures that children enjoy, coloring books and crayons, or soothing music.

- **Problem-solving with kids.** Problem-solving is another skill you want to help your kids develop. Realistically speaking, you will not always be able to be there telling them what they should do. As parents, you can encourage them to create some solutions with your support, guide them to solutions in line with the right values that take other people's feelings into consideration.
- **Identifying mood boosters.** Discuss and talk to your kid about the things they love to do and make them feel happy, such as singing their favorite songs or reading a joke book. Write down these things and let them know these are their mood boosters.

6. Avoid Reinforcing Kids' Outbursts

Sometimes, parents will inadvertently encourage their children to have emotional outbursts. The ways you respond to your kid's emotions and behaviors will make a big difference. If you're working on assisting your kids manage their emotions better, it's best to **avoid** the following:

- **Tell your kid to stop crying**. This can only make them more upset. If your child sees you getting worked up over their tears, they may think they might have done something wrong, which will not make it any easier to stop the crying.

- **Reward kids for calming down**. If you offer them a special treat every time they pull themselves together, they would learn that tears are useful to get something they want.
- **Calm kids down constantly**. Offering reassurance is helpful, but you also need to teach kids the skills to calm down by themselves so that they can manage their emotions when you're not there to help.
- **Shower your kids with attention**. Although it's important to offer comfort to them, make sure don't overdo it. You won't want your kids to learn that getting upset is the easiest way to get your attention.
- **Announce that they're sensitive**. Some parents may warn every teacher, friend's parent, or coach that your kid is sensitive, which will send the message that he/she cannot handle the feelings. Only consider offering this information if you think it can provide some insights or allow them to change their approaches to interacting with your kid. At the same time, be sure you say it positively, like "My kid feels big emotions."

1.4 Two often asked questions answered

1. When to challenge your kids

There may be several times when you think it makes sense to spare your kid from upsetting events. However, you don't want to excuse them from tough challenges or all the life realities.

Kids also need to practice how to manage their emotions in a socially appropriate way. They shouldn't miss out on life just because they can be overly emotional. Usually, emotional children experience all emotions in a relatively big way, which can mean your child may also enjoy the positive emotions, including excitement or happiness, to their fullest extent too. You won't want to squash your kids' abilities to feel all of these big emotions.

2. When should seek professional help

Sometimes, the children who are not usually overly emotional can go through a period when tears just keep coming. When you feel there's no other likely reason for this, it's worth checking in with the pediatrician. Especially for young children, if you found they have a hard time communicating, check-in with professionals to make sure there's no undetected language problem or an undiagnosed ear infection.

After the medical problems rule out, you can help kids learn how to manage their emotions at the big times, so it won't become an issue for them as they grow up.

If your kid has always been emotional, there is probably no reason to concern. However, if they suddenly seem to have more difficulties handling emotions, talk to the pediatrician.

If you find their emotions are causing problems for their daily life, you also should seek professional help for your kids. For example, they cannot concentrate in class because they're crying so much at school or struggling to maintain friendships because of their inability to control emotions. Your kids may need some extra help and support.

Research has discovered the association between dysregulation and various mental health issues as kids grow up, including depression, anxiety, substance abuse, attention deficit hyperactivity disorder (ADHD), suicide ideation, etc. Researches also stated that the interventions designed for self-regulatory behaviors could help kids better solve these problems. So don't hesitate to talk

to pediatricians or other related professionals
about your concerns.

2. Engaging Cooperation

"What can I do with this kid? When everyone wants to play outside, he throws a tantrum. When I ask him if he's ready for dinner, he always says no. When other kids are working on a science project, he just doesn't want to do it. When will this kid learn to cooperate?"
— A frustrated caregiver

Need to get your kids to:

- Go to sleep
- Go potty
- Get dressed
- Get in the car
- Clean up their toys
- Come to eat their dinner

With a bit more ease?

We all know how hard it can be to get kids to respond to our requests.

Cooperation means that a person is able to think about the balance his/her needs and wants with another person's. We often think of as cooperation as kids doing what adults want. That's not the case. True cooperation means a joint effort- a give and take between people that ends up with something mutually satisfying. Cooperation is a must-learned skill.

2.1 Pediatrician-Recommended Ways To Get Kids To Cooperate

1. Grab Kids' Attention

Just like your kids ask for your undivided attention before they do a cartwheel, you need to command your kids' attention if you expect them to listen.

If your kid hasn't brushed his teeth after you've asked him to multiple times. Likely, he didn't pay enough attention and didn't realize you were talking to him.

Studies show that the likelihood of kids' cooperating is influenced by what they're doing when the parent makes the request. Before the pediatricians begin the physical exam, they always ensure that their little patients are not busy with other things like the game or toy, make eye contact, and then speak directly to them, whatever the patient's age is. If the kids are actively looking at you, their cooperation chances will go up.

So when you need a task done from them next

time, make sure your kid isn't in the middle of doing other activities before talking. For example, near bedtime, look your kid in the eye and give a warm-up direction, "It's almost time for bed." Once he/she makes eye contact, quickly give the actual instructions, "It's time to brush your teeth now and get ready for sleep."

2. **Don't ask, Tell.**

You may think you can get a better response from children if you ask them politely to follow what you said, but this isn't the case. Children are not like adults, and they simply don't understand your polite question actually means "Do this."

Rather than saying, "could you please pick up your toys?" it's likely to get a better response by saying, "put away your toys now." According to the result of a study of 3-7 year olds, suggestions like "Can you put your shoes on?" do not get the same results as clear directions such as, "Put your shoes on." The study also stated that kids usually cannot fully understand irony or sarcasm until around ten years old. So it's very likely to fail to work by using those too.

It's also helpful if you can learn from the ways your kids communicate. Pay attention to what they used to ask their friends to do something, and compare the words or phrases to how you can express the same request. Try to use their same words or phrases the next time you want them to sit down, eat dinner, or clean up their rooms. If you find this doesn't work, consider dialing down your own vocabulary. Speak in simple words and phrases, or say the exact same thing in two different ways; your kids will be able to understand you better and may learn a new word.

3. **Clown around.**

Kids are much more likely to surrender to parents or their doctors when they're funny. Dr. Karen Carson, M.D., a pediatrician in New Mexico, turns his physical exam into a silly scavenger hunt. He tells his patients that he sees Dory, or Elmo in their ears, elephants in the tummy, or monkeys in the mouth. You can apply Dr.Carson's trick in all kinds of situations. For example, when you are trying to wipe your little one's face and he is wiggling or fighting, tell a story about how the princess should be clean to go to the castle. Look for characters, tell a story, sing or make funny noises. You will find the struggles stopped, and your kid goes along with the fun too.

4. **The Choice Trick**

"Do you want to wear the black sweater or the red one" Choices can work effectively when kids do not want to be told what to do. This technique will work great as long as both choices end in what you want your kids to do. Usually, they will pick one, and then you can move on. If your kid refuses to pick, that's your cue to say, "Then Mommy will pick for you. "

What if you cannot give your kid another option? It will also be helpful if you can explain your thinking. For instance, when you want your kid to put on the sunscreen, instead of simply saying, "No.", you can explain that we have to block the ultraviolet rays from the sun to prevent cancers, and you will find they are more willing to cooperate. Also, encourage your kids to share their own thinking, which will help them learn another critical social skill-negotiation. Let's say your daughter wants to skip her drawing practice today. Rather than refuse her request directly, let her tell her rationale. You can give her a pass if she offers a good argument, such as promising to practice extra later in the week or wanting to spend time with the family. Remember, just do not relent if she begs and collapses to the floor, crying to get her way- this is not the negotiation skill you would like to reward.

5. **Have Patience.**

Kids are more likely to cooperate if they don't feel the rush, and they don't switch tasks quickly or easily as adults. If you get tired of repeating yourself, you probably only need to provide your child with more time to respond, which will be most likely to get you better results, eventually.

Research has shown that many parents usually don't give kids enough time to respond to the directions. Kristina Rober, a pediatric nurse at Johns Hopkins Hospital, uses the "going slow" tactic to get kids to take even the foulest medicine. According to her, if the child resists, she will administer the medicine one drop at a time. "A kid cannot spit out just one drop." She says. Besides, it's more efficient to be successful and slow than have to begin over after the little patient rejects the full dose.

So if you need to leave the house by 8 am, start your kid transitioning five or ten minutes prior. Just like any of us, kids like to know what to expect. Let them know what will happen, and don't rush them, allowing them to move to the next task at their own pace. They will be a lot more cooperative about what you want them to do.

If you want to speed this process a little bit, playing certain games with them can be a useful technique. For example, it usually takes forever to get your kid to walk from the elevator to the pediatrician's office; you can try playing the game "Red light, green light," which will give you total control over their pace.

6. Offer Specific Praise

When the kids do something well, pointing out the success will give them pride and confidence. When kids feel good about what they have done, they're much more likely to do more of it.

The general "you did so well" isn't enough for them to make the association between their cooperation and your compliment. The key is to give more task-specific praise. For example, you can say, "I noticed you brushed your teeth and put on your pajamas. I'm proud of you did that without me having to ask," rather than, "You're such a good kid."

Kids also love meeting their parents' expectations. Task-specific prase will make your kids much more likely to repeat the wanted task in the future.

2.2 30 Phrases For Encouraging Parent-Kid Cooperation

- What do you think the problem is?
- How can we solve this together?
- Let's try teamwork!
- What way would you fix it?
- Can you show me a different way to do it?
- What can we do together to move forward?
- Can you tell me more about your idea?
- I get it. How would you do it then?
- If we start over, what would you like to do differently?
- Would you like to help me?
- Let's rewind and try it again.
- May I help you?
- I understand. What should be our next step then?
- Can you show me your way?
- Let's try again. This time we can do it together.

- This time I will follow you, then you can follow me.
- Can you think of a solution?
- How about we take turns?
- I would love to hear your solutions.
- Would you like to hear my idea?
- Let's work together!
- Do you have any ideas you want to share?
- Would you like a helping hand?
- Can you show me how?
- What if we did this differently?
- This might work. Shall we try it then?
- This seems to be not working, but we can think of a way that can work together.
- What worked when we did this last time? Do we need to do it the same way?
- Do you have a way you want to try?
- Anyone want to pitch in?

3. Encouraging Autonomy

Our kids are unique with their own characters, feelings, temperaments, dreams, and tastes. Parents can offer opportunities for kids to take on responsibilities and make choices from a very young age. Encouraging autonomy leads to independence and self-determination. While this requires lots of patience, so be flexible and plan ahead.

3.1 What is Autonomy?

In its simplest sense, autonomy refers to the ability of a person to act on his or her own free will. When kids have the autonomy, it can help them build their self-esteem, confidence, and independence.

From the activities kids participate, to how they interact with peers, autonomy plays a role in almost everything kids do. Learning how to be independent is an essential and critical skill for all kids.

3.2 What about kids who have special medical needs?

For kids with chronic medical conditions or care needs, building autonomy is especially important. These kids usually feel powerless because they have to follow so many "rules" set by others, including their doctors, nurses and parents. If these kids are allowed to participate in their own care, they will have the chance to understand and learn the care better, which will help them feel more in control as well as build their self-esteem. These are the characteristics of resilient kids who are capable of facing new challenges positively.

Some kids need certain regular care, such as gastrostomy care or tracheostomy. In this case, parents can provide options related to the care, and just as importantly, offer the kids many reasonable choices in other areas of their life (e.g., Which color of clothing to wear, which toy they want to play with, etc.).

For the kids who do have limited autonomy (because they don't have the motor strength or control to carry out daily tasks or unable to understand), realistic options that can match their abilities can be offered to them.

3.3 How Autonomy Can Rock Kids World

When kids become more independent, they know how to express themselves and explore the world independently. Also, they will begin to understand how their actions and choices can affect the outcomes, what they do and do not have in control. Autonomy helps children develop a sense of self.

Most Important Ways That Autonomy Impacts kids' Development:

- **Cognitive Growth**

As kids make their own choices, they are actually solving problems. Their cognitive development grows when they think through the options presented to them. So making meaningful choices is a critical part of cognitive development.

- **Feeling in Control**

Although kids usually cannot be expected to be in total control of all their life aspects, they still need to feel that they have certain parts of their life in control to build confidence.

- **Building and Boosting Self-Esteem**

When kids feel they have ownership of certain things and can make their own choices, their self-esteem will be built or boosted. Being able to do something on one's own can foster a sense of achievement.

3.4 How to Encourage Kids' Autonomy

1. Spot the times when your kids don't need you

She is struggling with scooping foods, so you just take the spoon the do this for her. He is reading a book on his own, and you feel compelled to read with him each time. It can be so tempting to step in and be "useful."

"Mama! Mama!" sounds familiar?. Actually, kids will let you know when they really need your company. Observe them and see if they do need your help or company, or if they can better use the time to themselves.

2. Offer feedbacks only if needed

Part of encouraging autonomy includes no micromanaging. Allow your kids to stack the dishes north-south, even if you do them east-west. Giving feedbacks or being too critical is tempting, especially when you know they can do better. However, if done too much, or at the wrong time, you will discourage them from those activities. So if it will make little or no different, ultimately, learn to let it go.

But this doesn't mean no feedbacks, only offer

feedbacks for important things. There may not be a standard or correct way to stack dishes, and you can point out that they left oil residue or forgot to add dishwasher soap.

Also, when you try to correct the kids, do it encouragingly and positively, which won't berate their efforts.

3. Do one notch above what kids need help with

Just do one small nudge that can allow the kids to continue to finish it by themselves. For example, if your child is already independent with the potty, he needs your help to pull his pants up. Instead of pulling the pants up completely for him, just do one notch above what he needs help with.

Try to do one notch that can help kids do it on their own. The point is not to do the task entirely for them, but to help them enough to finish it by themselves.

4. Respect Opinions

Listen to your kids' opinions and ideas. This will help develop their sense of autonomy. Respecting their opinions shows to them that their input on the world around them does matter. It also demonstrates that adults respect and recognize their abilities.

5. Offer choices

Letting kids to make their own choices is one of the most important steps to encourage their autonomy. If possible, set up an environment with many available options. For instance, allow kids to decide whether they want to play independently or with other friends.

6. Provide responsibilities

Give kids really responsibilities that matter. These tasks should be somewhat challenging to help them develop perseverance—for example, gardening, dishwashing, or cooking from a recipe. Assign your kids something to help them feel they are performing adult-like responsibilities.

7. Do not redo your kids' work

Let's say if you taught your daughter how to make her bed with all the tips you could think of to get the sheets smooth. But after she did it by herself, you found she didn't do exactly as you taught her and missed some tips you think can help her sleep more comfortably. Will you redo the bed for her?

Actually, if the bed she made does bother her, she will learn to fix it. Also, she will feel having more ownership and pride with her "not that neat" bed than if you fixed it in your way. Sometimes you just need to back off and allow them to do things in their way.

3.5 Examples in Action

Here are some examples to get you brainstorming. Please remember to get your kids involved in the process. They can have great ideas for how they can take even more responsibilities.

- **Kid Autonomy – Eating Alone**

Most children can take part in feeding themselves by nine months of age. When they are age two or three, they are capable of full self-feeding. By the age of five, kids can help set and clear the table. Many children will be able to pack their lunches or make a simple meal by age six. Not only can kids have more autonomy during the eating process, but they will eat better. As your kids participate more in preparing meals and mealtime, the mealtime battles will decrease. You could try playing sous-chef to make this task easier. Make sure your kids can get everything they need to feed themselves. In the lower refrigerator shelf or drawer, create a snack center. Also, create a shelf in the pantry that includes everything they may need to pack the lunches. A little preparation in advance reduces frustration and increases your kids' success rate.

- **Kid Autonomy – Getting Dressed**

Most children can participate in dressing themselves by the age of three. When they're six, most of them will be able to dress from head to toe. By the age of eight, most kids can wash and fold the clothes. Self-dressing is considered a fantastic "chore" because it allows for personal expression, ownership of self and usually can free up some time for the busy parents in the morning. Please store the clothes in a way that your kids can access easily. Emphasize options as much as possible. It is a good thing that the rules of fashion do not restrain kids. Streamline other morning routines so that you can give kids the extra time they may need to complete this task independently.

- **Kid Autonomy – Cleaning Up**

Most children will be able to clean up by age one. Actually, dump and clean is a game for children, and they will enjoy it. Do cleaning up can become a good habit even before children understand what "chore" is. You can help them by utilizing small bins which can be moved around the room and easier to be filled up. Encourage this activity by making sure it happens regularly- after each activity, children will not feel overwhelmed by cleaning the whole room later.

- **Kid Autonomy – Getting in the Car Safely**

By the age of two, most children are able to climb into their own seats. When they are five, most kids can buckle themselves safely and securely. At the age of six, most of them can assist siblings in the process. This activity allows kids to feel incredibly accomplished. When they can properly secure the five-point harness for the first time, their smile will light up the car. Also, this gives the parent more time to load the car. To make time for this "chore," get the kids in the car first and then load your other stuff, which will give them the time and space to accomplish their task. Consider installing Lulabocs or LulaClips in your car to make it more kid-friendly. Don't forget to emphasize that some difficulties are part of the learning process. Rather than praise their outcomes, prase their efforts to encourage them to keep trying and working when it's challenging. Offer your help when they need it.

- **Kid Autonomy – Laundry**

Most children are capable of help you stuff the washing machine and start it by the age of two. When children are at the age of four, they are able to help sort and fold the laundry. At the age fix, they can put away their clothes. They can handle this task from beginning to end by age eight. Let your children help you out. Similar to other tasks, modify the space allowing kids' independence. Choose the detergent that they can safely handle. Put the step stool for them in the right place if needed. Don't forget to allow imperfection and prase your kids' efforts.

This could be the most important thing you do as a parent.

There's a connection between childhood chores and academic achievement as well as mental health. It could be challenging at first to make the time, efforts, and space for your children to complete these activities, but remind yourself they're not just chores, and they are critical life lessons too. Compared to those expensive sports participation or fancy music lessons, you can foster double your kids' resilience and self-esteem by training them to do the chores. Of course, there's an immediate payoff - can ease your load as the parent.

Section 2

Get Your Kids to Listen

1. Empowering Ways To Get Kids To Listen

1. Say it with a single word

The scenario: The girl has only one assigned chore: to carry her plates to the sink when she finished eating. While still, not one night went by when the mom doesn't need to tell her to do it, sometimes need multiple times. Even this wouldn't guarantee they would, and guess who would end up with clearing them?

The old way: After the girl ignored the mom's repeated requests, the mom sits her down and preach for minutes about how the parent is not her servant, and this is not a restaurant.

The better way: Usually, kids know what they

are supposed to, while they just need simple reminders. Instead of repeated preaching, try to use one word to jog their memory.

Results: After dinner, all the mom said was one word: “plates.” At first, the girl looked at the mom as if she were peaking in an alien tongue. However, a second later, the girl picked up the plates and headed for the kitchen. After about a month of reinforcement, the mom doesn’t need to say anything, and the girl would do it automatically. Other examples: using “Shoes!” to replace “find your shoes and put them on”; using “Teeth!” to get them to brush their teeth.

2. Provide Information

The scenario: After the mom just served the dinner when, as usual, her 3-year-old Blair jumped off her chair, stood, turned around, just wouldn't sit.

The old way: “How hard is it to understand? You must sit down!” the mom gets annoyed and said. Blair would cry while still wouldn’t sit. As a result, she got a time-out, which still didn’t change her behavior.

The better way: Instead of keeping issuing commands, state the facts. Nobody won’t rebel against constant orders. The kids are not robots programmed to do our commands. They have the desire and need to exercise their free will, which is why they usually do exactly the opposite of what you asked them to. Can you guess what the trick is? It's to turn your order into the teaching moment. This method says to the kid, "I know that when you get all the information, you will choose to do the right thing." For example, instead of saying, "put that juice way," you may say, "Juice will spoil when left out."

The Result: When Blair is playing jungle gym at mealtime, the mom said calmly, "chairs are meant for sitting." Blair smiled at her, sat down, and then began to eat. Although the mom still needs to remind Blair now and then, Blair would listen in the end. This approach can be applied to other situations too. For example, instead of saying "stop touching the vase", you can say, "The glass is delicate and can break very easily. "

3. State Your Expectations

The scenario: The mom allowed her kid Everly to watch TV before they left for school, and she was preparing for the school stuff. After everything is ready, Everly was still not getting ready to turn off the TV and whined,"

Just five more minutes. Pleeeeeeeese!"

The old way: Mom would get upset and yell," No, That's it, you have watched enough." Everly would keep asking for more time, and the mom would keep yelling," I said no!"

The better way: Tell your children and let them know your plan ahead of time. The mom can say, "After you brush your teeth and get dressed, you can watch a little more TV while I'm preparing the school stuff. Then you will be able to arrive at school on time."

The Result: When the mom first tried this technique, Everly turned off the TV without saying a word. But the next morning, Everly refused and started delaying again. The mom quickly realized she forgot to remind Everly of the plan ahead of time this morning. So for the following morning, she re-stated it clearly, "When I finish packaging, I expect you to turn off the TV." Another success.

4. Give Your kids the choice

The scenario: When a family is playing on the beach, the mom is going to put some sun screen on her 6-year old Dane, but he refused.

The old way: The mom ended up yelling after

repeatedly try to persuade him to cooperate, "If you don't put it on, you will not be allowed to play in the water." Dane bawls his eyes out, and then no one would have any fun at the beautiful beach.

The better way: Provide your kids with choices. Nobody will like threats or punishments, and they just won't work. Instead of feeling sorry for not cooperating, the kids will be more likely to become even more stubborn. However, if you make him part of the decision, he will have a much higher chance to follow what's acceptable to you.

The result: The mom offers," Dane, you can put on the sunscreen now or before you're going to play under the sun. " Dane still doesn't respond. But after he saw other boys and girls running around and playing in the water, the mom said, "Dane, here's your sunscreen.", and he put it right on.

2. How to Get Your Kids to Listen the First Time You Speak

Feeling Ignored By Your Kids?

Whether your kid tunes you out when he keeps banging on the table after you told him to stop or you told him to pick up his toys, getting your kids to listen can sometimes feel like an uphill battle. Especially nowadays, getting kids to listen can be even more challenging than ever before in our digital world. You are competing against video games, TV, and many other distractions to capture your kids' attention. Surely, electronics are not the only reason your kids don't listen and follow directions. They can also tend to have selective hearing.

Now let's talk about the simple changes you can make to the way you give directions in order to get your kids to listen the first time you speak.

- **Be sure your kids really hear you and get rid of distractions.**

When you give them instructions, shouting up the stairs or across the house while your kids are playing video games or scrolling through social medial does not count.

Research has reported that kids engaged in activities, for example, gaming, reading, or playing, usually won't register other aspects of their surroundings. What they lack here is called "peripheral awareness." A limited peripheral awareness will prevent kids from registering what's happening around them like a parent is talking to them and just standing close by.

Before attempting to give directions or make a request, get rid of any distractions. Begin by saying, "Please pause your game so that I can talk to you." or "I can see you're busy now. Will there be a few-minute break so we can talk?" After you get your kids' full attention, give your instructions. When you find your kids struggle to put down their electronics or pause their show, work on that behavior first. If they cannot disengage as you tell them it's time to take a break, tell them you will take away their electronics privileges.

For younger kids, kneel down in front of them and make eye contact when giving your instructions. It's also helpful to give them a positive physical connection, like a friendly touch on the arm. For older kids, try a minimum of eye contact and the acknowledgment that they can hear you. For the kids with ADHD, a hand on the shoulder can be an extra help to make sure you have their full attention.

- **If you find your kids ignore you on purpose.**

Some kids will "test" the parents to see what will happen if they just ignore you. This is normal during the development. Consider that you may have taught them unintentionally in the past that you can be ignored.

- **Don't ask, tell.**

It's common for parents to give directions mistakenly by asking, not telling. For example, when you ask," Could you please clean your room?" even a slightly oppositional kid can say, "No!" Instead, say directly, "Please clean your room now."

Whenever possible, give your kid a five-minute warning. Rather than saying, "Go pick up your toys now," when your kid is in the middle of playing, say, "In five minutes, you need to stop playing and pick up your toys."

After the five minutes passed, say, "Now it is time to stop playing and pick up your toys."

This is to show respect to your kids and give them time to be prepared to switch activities.

- **One instruction, one time.**

Younger children, especially those children with attention problems, usually will not respond to several directions at once well. It can cause your kids to miss a step or two along the way by saying, "Pick up your socks, put your backpack away, and put your dirty shirts in the washing machine."

Begin with one direction at a time. Before you give them another new one, wait until your kids finish the first task. For those older kids or teenagers, they may be able to handle several instructions at a time, and they should be capable of working their way through a list. You can say things like, "It's time to do your chore list." Your kids can accept responsibility for finish every task on the list.

- **Let your kids repeat your instructions.**

Ask your kids to repeat back what they heard after you give them the instructions. Repeating can make sure your kids understand your expectations, and it also provides you a chance to clarify if there's any confusion.

Sometimes, they may say "OK," while they have no idea what you talked about. Or, you may discover that they need an explanation about what to do. If you find they cannot understand, repeat your directions until they do.

- **Reinforce positive behaviors.**

Provide positive consequences to reinforce your kids' good behaviors when your kids follow your instructions. Praise them by saying, "Great job picking up your toys when I asked you to." Also, if your kids have done an excellent job listening, offer them a surprise reward once in a while. You can also consider establishing a formal token economy or reward system to motive them to keep up the great work.

- **Give them a fair warning or a negative consequence for the non-compliances.**

This is what will happen if they don't respond to your directions. Consider a single "if…then" warning if your kids don't follow your directions. Say something like, "if you don't pick up your toys right now, you cannot play with them for the rest of the day."

Fair warning is important because kids know in advance what's the negative consequence will be for ignoring a request or breaking a rule. They are making decisions about their behaviors: whether to break the rule and bear the negative consequences or follow the rules.

When your kids don't comply, take away a privilege, like toys or electronics, for up to 24 hours. At the same time, give your kids a chance to respond. If they don't do what you asked, and it's a reasonable direction, the next step will be to follow the consequences you have previewed for them.

After you gave your kids negative consequences for not following instructions, they should learn that you are serious the first time you speak. And they will become more compliant with your directions over time.

3. Correcting Behaviors In Kids Who Won't Listen

It can be very frustrating when your kids seem not to be listening, or even worse, appear to ignore you outright. You might wonder if your kids are rebellious or if you're doing something wrong. In fact, there are a couple of reasons why kids don't listen; for example, they haven't got the skill yet.

No matter what challenges you are experiencing regarding your kids' listening skills, it's beneficial to understand some reasons behind their inability to listen. It also helps to have a few strategies up your sleep to build better listening skills in your children.

3.1 Why Kids Don't Listen

As parents, it's overwhelming sometimes to get reluctant kids to listen. It's natural to think about listening behaviors in terms of respect: if my kids don't pay attention and don't listen, it's a disrespect sign.

The truth is failing to listen is not always about respect. It's a development stage kids go through as they also try to sort out their world. It might feel like disrespect, but it's probably about something more basic. Kids can struggle to listen because you are coming off as complaining or critical or your instructions are too long. It can also be challenging for kids to listen if your messages are inconsistent or complicated.

In some other situations, displaying the inability to focus or failing to listen is tied to something else like a mental or hearing health issue. However, more often than not, it's more about your kids' social development than about anything else when your kids fail to listen effectively.

Even knowing that the kids' inability to listen is more likely developmental, it still can be unnerving as you feel like the television, playtime, or video games seem to be more important than what you need to say.

3.2 What to do When Your Kids Ignore You

The techniques mentioned in the previous sections also work here, including requesting repetition, giving one fair warning, rewarding good listening, etc. There are additional steps that will help when your kids don't listen.

- **Be consistent.**

When the messages the kids receive are consistent, they learn best. So be sure your expectations about listening behaviors are consistently and clearly communicated. Your kids need to know what is working and expected to become a more active listener.

Even though it's critical to be patient, you won't want to give your kids mixed signals regarding the importance of listening. By communicating your expectations and interacting with your kids consistently, you will eventually start to see positive changes in your kids' listening skills.

- **Create a plan.**

Instead of accusing them of not listening, try to have a conversation regarding the possible roadblocks. Make your concerns understood by saying, "I see we are having a difficult time getting things done. What do you think is getting in the way of you being able to follow through?"

It's enough for some kids to be motived to keep up the good work by receiving positive attention and praise. If you point out to your kid, "Excellent job picking up the toys when I asked you to," they may feel more motivated to repeat this behavior.

For some other kids, they need a bigger incentive to follow directions. Consider a token economy system or a reward system to motive your kids to be more compliant.

- **Figure out underlying issues.**

If you find your kids refuse to listen is a problem in more than one environment, such as both at school and home, it's critical to rule out any underlying issues. Before you assume your kids are ignoring you, there are several questions you should ask yourself:

Do your kids have a cognitive condition? Cognitive impairments or developmental problems can make it challenging for kids to process information and take action in a short time.

Do your kids have trouble paying attention? If your kids are not able to focus long enough to follow through with what you've said, or your kids mainly focus on what they're doing and they don't hear you, they might have a condition such as Attention Deficit Hyperactivity Disorder (ADHD).

Do your kids have a hearing issue? If your kids appear to have trouble hearing you or understating your instructions, get your kids' hearing checked.

If you doubt that your kids may have an underlying mental or medical health issue, talk to their pediatrician. The pediatricians can assess your kids and rule out any mental or medical health explanation for their behaviors. If an underlying problem is diagnosed, you will be capable of working with them on treatments.

- **Model good communication skills.**

There are several benefits to encourage your kids' listening skills. First, kids learn far more from what they saw than what they heard, so be sure you are modeling the behaviors you would like to see. Second, you show them respect as you make time to listen to their concerns. It then will be easier for them to show respect back when they feel respected.

Kids will mimic your listening behaviors when they learn more about interpersonal communications. When your kids are ready, take the time to talk to them, it will be more likely for them to respond to you when you need them to listen.

- **Avoid traps.**

Parents sometimes inadvertently train their kids to ignore them. Nagging, yelling, and begging are more likely to make kids ignore you. Giving too many commands or lengthy lectures will also stop your kids from listening.

Consider reserving your instructions for the most important issues you would like to address. Whenever possible, stick to a single warning since repeating warnings will let your kids think that they don't need to listen the first time you speak.

3.3 Discipline: Top Don'ts and Do's When Your Kids Don't Listen

As you tried to ask your kids to do some tasks, you have tried all the tricks: counted to three, used the "mom or dad voice," and broke out all the stops while your kids still defy you.

It's enough to make parents feel frustrated! When you be serious and discipline your kids, do you know where do you draw the line? Are you sure if you're disciplining them correctly?

Here are some top don'ts and dos for you to follow as you discipline your little one.

- **Don't consider discipline as punishment**

Discipline can sound like you're punishing your children. But it's more of a way of engaging actively with children to help mold their moral characters. Discipline is an approach to teach them right from wrong and is a skill that is critical to function in society.

We are teaching our kids restraint and self-control with discipline. While punishment is a loss of privilege or a direct, pointed penalty that serves as retribution. However, discipline is far more effective compared to punishment, knowing that it can require a little more work. Also, remember that it's a process.

- **Do set limits and stick to them**

As adults, we all have to abide by limits, and our kids need to understand these boundaries too. Spend your time teaching them to know the appropriate behaviors you expect from them. While if you set your limits, make sure to stick to it. One of the examples is setting a curfew.

If your kids falter, they need to know that there will be expected, consistent consequences. There will be no new negotiations, surprises, nor retractions.

- **Do find opportunities for praise**

It's vital to pay attention to what your kids are doing and recognize that aloud to them. Make efforts to notice when your kids are actively engaged in appropriate behaviors, praise and compliment them accordingly. Offering positive attention to good behaviors can go a long way. It not only can help build their confidence in themselves but mold their behaviors too.

Take the time to listen carefully to what your kids said and agree when appropriate. Just say no if you disagree while ensuring you take the time to let them know the reasons. Be the role models and show your empathy. Communication is always the key.

- **Do be specific**

It can cause frustrations for both you and your kids when your kids are not clear about what you expect, but you assume they should know. So, set realistic and clear limits with your kids. Also, be specific with goals.

It's too general and broad to say," you'd better be good." Be specific with your instructions and let them know exactly what "good" looks like, helping them understand what's expected from them. For example, being good may mean not running through a crowded airport or not interrupting a speaking adult.

- **You are their parent, instead of their buddy**

It can be tempting to treat your kids like your good friends. However, your kids need you to teach and lead them as they grow. Setting limits and disciplining your kids will instill confidence as they learn to navigate through their lives. We are actively involved as teachers during the discipline, not just the passive observers suddenly required to react. It requires work and is an ongoing process.

While disciplining can pay dividends as you watch your little ones grow, develop a good moral compass and get more confident.

Family communication can be one of the most challenging things parents need to handle. It takes time, consistency, and patience to teach your kids to become good listeners. While if you make efforts, your kids can become good communicators and active listeners, which is a skill that will benefit them for the rest of their lives.

Section 3

How To Talk to Kids

1. How To Talk To Kids

As parents, especially new parents, you must have some moments worrying about how to talk to these small people. Even if you don't have children, there may be times when you need to engage with them; for example, you're sitting next to your cousin's son at the family reunion. You can do it. If kids feel you are genuinely interested in them, they can be wonderful conversationalists. Here are some tips that will help.

- **Call them by their names**

Don't use the names like "little Princess" or "little Dude," which is basic respect. Kids are just like us, and they need to be addressed by their names to feel respected.

- **Don't need to change your voice.**

The higher-pitched sing-song tone may be responded well by babies. However, with kids over three years old, you just need to talk like yourself. Kids will respond best to people who just talk to them as they talk to anyone else. When you speak with children, you may use simpler phrases but don't need to dumb down your words.

- **Get down to kids' level physically.**

It might be hard to get up, while it's a nice gesture to show the kids that you're not above them. This is also a good way to enable you to talk with them eye-to-eye.

- **Name-drop familiar children's interests in those casual conversations.**

Rather than ask a child, "Have you been to Disneyland?", try to slip in familiar kid-interests in your stories. "Once, I was riding the Teacups at Disneyland. I spun so fast that I felt so dizzy." The child's eye will light up, thinking "I felt dizzy too when on the teacup ride." It's more likely for children to jump in with their own interesting stories.

- **Get resourceful.**

Do you have something that may be interesting in your bag? Get your phone, open Instagram stories and go to the selfie mode, put some funny face filters on the kid. They love funny face filters.

- **Show children your scars if you have.**

We are not talking about the ones that you had a breakup with your ex-boyfriend several years ago. Your actual scars. Show children your scar and share with them how you got it. Children usually like showing off their own scars, so your behavior lets them know that you are interested in listening to their stories about how they got them.

- **Avoid those cheap tricks.**

These cheap tricks include having them see how hard they can punch your hands, trying to get children to open up by tickling them, and asking them if they have a girlfriend or boyfriend. Also, don't start by saying how pretty or cute they are.

- **Just be yourself.**

Like adults, kids look to the other person for cues on how to act. Therefore, if you feel uncomfortable, they will feel too. While when you talk with them like any other people naturally, they will open up. If they open up, listen. You may even learn something new.

2. How to Talk to Kids about Difficult Topics

It may be one of the most challenging parenting jobs to talk to kids about difficult subjects. It can feel impossible to put into words those really big issues, for example, drugs, racism, violence, or other weighty topics. However, in the age of 24-hour news coverage, streaming videos, and cell phone notifications, even little kids are exposed to those serious stories. So it's important to face this challenge in advance. If you can address the tough stuff and teach them about the world appropriately, your bond with children will be strengthened and your kids feel safer. If they learn how to ask questions, and cross-check sources, gather and interpret information, they will become critical thinkers. Confronting the issues the world wasn't able to solve is sad. However, we can provide them all the tools they will need to make things better by investing in kids with compassion, strong character, and knowledge.

Most parents get the deer-in-the-headlights

feeling as the kids learn about something unsettling or scary, such as suicide on TV shows, graphic porn by Google research, or a mass shooting. But it's always a good idea to consider their developmental or age stage when you begin the conversations since kids absorb information in a different way from babies to teens. For instance, younger children are literal. They will fly across the room to avoiding getting ankles munched if you tell them there's a monster under the bed. If you tell your teen kids the same thing, they will tell you to take a flying leap. So it's helpful to understand how kids perceive the words in every development stage so that you can deliver information about those difficult topics in the most age-appropriate way. While each kid brings his or her own temperament, sensitivities, experience, and other individual traits to any conversations. So use your best judgment and observe how your kids tend to receive information to decide how deep to go.

The following are the tips for discussing any difficult subjects with kids from 2 years old to teen based on child development guidelines.

Age 2 - 6

At this age stage, kids don't have enough life

experience to understand some elements in those difficult, complex topics. Also, they don't a firm grasp on cause and effect as well as abstract concepts. For them, themselves and their primary relationships (parents, grandparents, siblings, or/and family pets) are their world's center, and they tend to focus on how things affect them. These kids can be sensitive to parents' emotional states and will worry if they did something that made you upset. It becomes tough to explain big topics to them due to all of these. Besides, it would help if you managed their media exposure, and they often move on very quickly.

- **Reassure with both gestures and words**: You could say, "You are safe. Daddy and Mommy are safe too." Snuggling and hugs will also work wonders.
- **Keep the news at bay**. Try your best to limit your little kids' exposure to age-inappropriate subjects by muting or turning off the TV and selecting the media that targets their age.
- **Adress both their and your feelings**. You may say, "It's okay to feel sad, confused, or scared. They are natural, and we all have those feelings."

- **Find out what they knew**. The kids at this age might not understand those issues well. So ask them what they think happened before you do your talk.
- **Catch your own biases**. Rather than saying "homeless lady," "black boy," or "fat guy," say, "woman," "man," "boy," and "girl." Avoid describing people's weight, sexual identity, ethnicity, financial status, etc., unless it's relevant to the issues.
- **Use basic feelings terms like "afraid," "sad," "mad," "happy," and "surprised."** They cannot understand mental illness totally, even though they can understand emotions. So you can say that someone is confused too much or angry too much and need extra help. Avoid using idiomatic expressions, for example, "flew the coop." or "blew a gasket."
- **Use ideas, vocabulary, and relationships they are familiar with.** Try to recall a similar and recent situation from their lives that they are able to relate to. For example, "A man has stolen something. Remember someone took your lunchbox?"
- **Communicate that someone is in charge.** For instance, "The police will catch that bad guy." or "Daddy and

Mommy will make sure nothing bad happens to us."

Age 7 - 12

Children in this age group can write and read, and they would get exposed to age-inappropriate content more accessible and more often. However, children at this age are still kind of shaky on what's pretend and real. After kids gain real-world experience, abstract-thinking skills, and the ability to express themselves, they can understand different perspectives and difficult subjects.

- **Wait for the right moment**. Kids are still likely to come to you when they hear something terrifying at this stage. You can feel them out to determine whether or not they want to discuss something. If they didn't bring it up, don't feel you have to broach those topics until they ask.
- **Create a safe discussion space**. Consider saying, "Those topics are tough to discuss even for adults. I won't be mad, and I would like you to feel free to ask anything you want."
- **Find out what they knew**. Ask your kids if their friends at school were talking about something or what they have

heard. Try not to over-explain and answer questions directly and simply.

- **Provide perspectives and context**. Children need to understand those issues' related circumstances to make sense of it fully. For race-based crimes, you can say, "Some people wrongly think that light-skinned people are better than those dark-skinned. They sometimes commit crimes unjustifiedly without the correct information." When a mass shooting happend, you can say, "The person who did this has problems in his brain that has confused his thoughts."
- **Be sensitive to kids' temperaments and emotions**. It's hard to know what will trigger your kids. So just check in by sharing your feelings and ask how they feel. For example, "I feel sad to hear that someone didn't get the right treatment to help him or good education." Or "It makes me feel angry when I know someone got hurt." And, "How do you feel now?"
- **Address their curiosity**. If you find your kid stumbles across grown-up material online, it may be the time to find some content allowing them to learn more about mature and age-appropriate subjects. For example, say, "Online

pornography is for some grown-ups to watch. However, it's not about romance or love and will give you some wrong ideas about sex. If you are interested in learning more about sex, I can give some resources to check, and we also can talk if any questions." If your child wants to explore the serious subjects deeper than you can offer, say, "Let's find some new resources providing current information for kids."

- **Look for positives**. Even though there might not be a silver lining to every cloud, but try to be optimistic. Say, "Let's try to find ways that we can help." Or "Many people acted like heroes at the crime scene."
- **Encourage critical thinking**. The open-ended questions can help kids think deeper about serious topics. Ask, "What did it make you think?", "What did you hear?", or "Why do you think that?" For the older kids, you can ask, "The news hyped up stories, so more people are going to pay attention. What do you think is the reason that this story is getting so much play?"

Teens

Kids at this age probably engage in the media independently. They can read, interact with, and even make their own and share what they learned in the form of memes, comments, and videos. Kids can hear about difficult topics in the news or from other places like social media, video game chats without your knowledge. At this stage, the kids are much more interested in what their friends think about the issue than your opinions. So ask questions prompting them to think through the arguments and encourage them to find media that can enrich their knowledge.

- **Encourage open dialogue**. Kids need to know that they can test their opinions, ask questions, and speak freely without fear of consequences. For example, "We may not agree on everything, but I would like to know what you are thinking."
- **Admit when you don't know something**. It's totally okay for kids to know that their parents might not know all the answers. For instance, "I don't know, but let's try to find out together."
- **Ask open-ended questions**. Such as, "What do you know about it?", "What do you think about the police brutality?", "Why do you think that?", or "Who do you think is at fault?"
- **Help them consider the complexities in difficult topics**. Issues like social

issues, tradition, politics can be complex; ask questions that can help them think through. For example, “What makes difficult issues, like violence, rape, and crimes so hard to solve?”, “How do policymakers can get to the issue’s bottom and current those tough issues?”, or “What key things will need to change to fix certain issues like poverty?”

- **Share your values**. Share where you stand on issues and explain the reasons you hold those values. For example, if you would like your kids to be respectful of other people’s differences, explain why you value acceptance and tolerance.
- **Ask what they will do if they were in a challenging situation**. Kids are trying to figuring out their own identities at this stage and can seek out risk. Thinking about how they will act when confronting with a terrible situation appeals to their sense of adventure, which can get them to grapple with ethical dilemmas and see themselves making good choices. Ask, “If you saw people being mistreated and you were caught in a political demonstration that turned violent, what will you do?”

- **Discuss kids' own news**. Social media like Instagram, Facebook and Twitter tend to serve up content from friends. Prompt them to consider how stories from social media differ from the ones supposedly objective news broadcasts on TV. Also, encourage them to consider how different sources put their spin on those issues and how those influence audiences' opinions. For instance, "Does a reporter need to experience heroin dependency to be able to report stories on opiate addiction?"
- **Get them to consider solutions**. Adolescents can be cynical but also can be idealistic. Let them know that you trust them for the future since if anything is going to get better, it's this generation who is going to do it. Say, "What issue will you solve first if you were in charge? why and how will you do it?"

3. How to Talk to Kids about Sexual Harassment

"What is sexual harassment? Mommy" You might hope that the news of some famous men being accused of sexual misconduct could fly right past your kid's radar. However, just like other unfortunate events, these pieces of news have a way to seep into your kids' world. Now, you may feel stuck: How do you talk about sexual harassment? How could you start if you haven't even talked about sex?

Talk one topic at a time. Consider tackling the sex angles and news separately. Younger children usually have a hard time understanding the abstract concepts. There's no reason to talk about sexual harassment specifically with very young children unless they ask about it. Be prepared if they bring it up.

- **Ask non-judgmental and open-ended questions**: This can allow you to get information about what you need to focus on, what you can skip, and what information you will need to correct.

Questions examples: "How did it make you feel to hear that?", "What do you think it is?", "Where did you learn that phrase?"

- **Remain reassuring and neutral**. Young kids can feel like it's their fault if the important adults in their lives are upset or angry. Even though it's obvious to you, it's still worth letting your kids know that you're not upset at them. Say something like, "This is a tough topic, but I'm happy you asked me about it." Or "It's always okay to share with me something even if you think it's something bad."
- **Explain the reason it's on the news**. It always helps to put matters in context even with small children who haven't grasped the concept of the 24-hour news cycle. Otherwise, they may feel confused and overwhelmed about the constant news coverage. If possible, turn the news off as young children are watching or listening. Instead, look for age-appropriate news sources. You can say, "Sexual harassment is against the law. It's like taking something that doesn't belong to you."
- **Be truthful while don't over-explain**. It's unnecessary to provide kids anything more than what they need to

know to satisfy their curiosity. Talking with words or phrases that you can understand, such as "private," "private parts," "bully." If your family uses "making babies," you can use it too. Say something like, "Sexual harassment is not appropriately talking about other people's or their own body or private parts. The sexual harasser sometimes will hug or touch other people without their permission."

- **Help them protect themselves as well as others**. Take the time to teach them about bullies and boundaries. Let them know their bodies are their own, and no one else has the right to touch them or talk about them in any way that makes them feel uncomfortable. Explain that they also must respect other people's right to keep their bodies private. For example, "If someone says something or touches your body, or if you see someone bullying someone else, what you should do is telling them to stop and report the adult in charge." Also, explain that your kids won't get in trouble for telling even though bullies told them they could not.

4. How to Talk to Kids about the Divorce

It's not an easy task to tell your kids about your divorce. You will need to have the conversation sooner or later. It can be the most challenging talk you will ever have with them even though you know it in your heart: divorce is the right decision for your family.

Telling kids about the changed family circumstances and divorce is overwhelming. While is there a way to make it less shocking? There is. Actually, the way you tell your kids will make a real difference in how they handle the divorce. Research over the past years also revealed that more than 75% of divorce parents talk to their kids about this for less than ten minutes in total. The following tips are meant to help you to be one of the parents in the healthiest 25%, to break the news as gently, but effectively as possible.

Tip #1 Have a Plan & Prepare in Advance

Divorce is nothing to take lightly. You must do the prep work when it comes to telling your kids. It's also essential that both you and your soon-to-be ex can be on the same page as do the talking.

Come up with a game plan. If possible, tell kids approximately two to three weeks before separation.

First, know what's your ultimate priority: The relationship between you and your spouse is ending, but not the relationship between you and the kids. Make sure your kids understand they are still loved and are going to continue to be cared for.

Then, be prepared for what questions your kids may ask and your answers to them. You are able to see the big picture and understand why divorce is the best choice, but your kids might have a more difficult time understanding.

Finally, not only think about when you are going to tell them about the divorce, but what's your plan to bring it up. Your toddler will take the news differently than your teen, so it's vital to know how to talk to them based on their age and development stage.

Preschool (Age 2-5)

Parents tend to assume that children this young are the least affected by the divorce news. Will they even remember it? However, preschool-aged children depend on their parents for almost everything – shelter, food, stability, and love! The divorce news will not only rock them significantly, but they are at a self-focused age where they may think the divorce is their fault. They might make the leap from mom left dad to mom left me.

Remind your kids of their own importance and give them the reassurance they need. They will be cared for and loved by both of their parents. Support a two-home concept as well as nix the idea of "our house" and "mom's house." Your children will benefit most by considering both houses as homes because this is exactly what they are.

At the same time, prepare to answer many questions over time. It's hard for little children to grasp this concept, so it's critical to be patient and help them understand in their way and time.

What to Watch For: Distress signs in preschoolers include anger, fear, or emotional instability, which could be expressed indirectly through anxiety, clinginess, whininess, or general irritability. They might also begin to lose ground in their developments. For example, children who were able to sleep through the night begin to wake up more often.

Young Children (Age 5-9)

Children at this age may be more in tune with handling bigger emotions. However, it can still be hard for them to understand the divorce fully. They also can fall into the trap of blaming themselves for it. Did mom move out because she's upset at me? Did Dad leave because I misbehaved? So be ready to discuss how they feel about the news. Are they anxious? Sad? Or angry? It's beneficial for you to talk them through what's on their mind and develop concrete ideas on how you can help manage those feelings.

What to watch for: Children at this age may show their distress as anxiety, fear, sadness, anger. Some may have fantasies about reconciliation and think about what they can do to make it happen. While some display more clear-cut signs of missing their absent parent. According to the psychologist, Dr. Freeman, children who still think that they somehow caused the divorce or what they can do to bring their parents back together will have trouble getting on with the healing process. So what they need to understand is that this is adult decision which they didn't contribute to and cannot influence.

Older Kids (Age 10 and up)

Kids at this stage have a greater understanding of divorce. However, since they've spent so many years under one roof and now it's going to change, so it can feel as though they have the most to lose.

You will be able to be more specific. Explain clearly what divorce means and how custody works. While more in-depth questions might come with greater details. So be ready to give them truthful answers.

Simultaneously, don't forget to mention that their relationship with you won't change. It doesn't hurt to remind them that divorce is an adult concept, and parents don't divorce their kids.

What to watch for: Anger and irritability are common at one of the moved-out parent or both. It can be difficult to gauge how much of the young teen's moodiness is caused by the divorce. Think back to what your teen was like before the separation and how his/her mood and behavior changed. This may give you a clue to the cause.

Tips #2 Break the News Together

Divorce is a family matter as kids are involved. Be simple and plain. Both parents need to prepare to work as a team. Try to be ready to do this when you are unlikely to become angry with each other or lose your temper.

On the other side, even you it's tempting to pull your oldest ones aside and told them the news before their younger siblings. However, this will do more harm than good. If possible, gather everyone together and share the news at the same time.

Tip #3 Talk in a Quiet Space

Talk to your kids in a quiet space and when there is nothing that needs to be done later. So if possible, do it at weekends and the start of the weekends are the best since you will be around them to be close to and talk to during the immediate days after the talk.

Tip #4 Consider Notifying Their Teachers in Advance

Tell their teachers the day before you talk to the kids in order to prepare the teachers for potential acting up or upset. Ask the teachers to understand and discreet the information, not to ask the kids anything about it, or mention it unless the kids bring it up.

Tip #4 Few Messages Worth Repeating

When you talk to the kids, there are several important messages to repeat – during the conversation and may in the months following:

1. This is something dad and mom have already decided after a long time of trying to make things work better.
2. Dad and Mom will both be happier.
3. It's an adult decision and has nothing to do with what the kids said or did, helping them understand they also cannot control this decision just by behaving "extra nicely."
4. Each of the parents will continue to be an important part of kids' lives, and kids can feel free to continue loving each parent fully without worry or fear of feeling disloyal or betraying the other parent. (This might be the toughest challenge for many parents. While it's vital if you want to protect kids from maladjustment or pain.)
5. It's normal to have different emotions. We all will feel angry, worried, sad, and maybe curious about the future. Parents need to be open to listening to all

feelings and offer help no matter how they feel.

6. There will be two homes where the kids will be loved. If one parent moves some distance away, reassure your kids that they can regularly see that parent. Also, explain how that might be accomplished.

Tip #5 Let Them Know The Plan If Possible

You don't need to very detailed, while you need to tell them the basics. For example, Who is going to stay in the house? Who will move out and about where? If the parent is still looking at houses/apartments, it's okay to invite the kids to come with you to check the new places. But if they don't want to come, it's also okay, just leave it alone. It's good to tell kids where the new place is when the parent found one. Let them know the basic plan: how often they will see each parent. Reassure that they will be with Mom sometimes and with Dad sometimes. However, don't promise anything you can't deliver.

Tip #6 Be Ready For A Second Conversation

After a few days after the first talk, if you know more of the plan's details, such as "Dad is going to drive you to school every day just like he did before." tell them this. For the things that will stay the same, let them know and reassure them that those things will remain as before. For those things that will be different: "Mom will drive you to school. It's different, but we will try to make that work. We will see how it's going, and you can let us know what is working and what is not."

Tip #7 Prepare For Any Reactions

Sometimes kids have tantrums and cry. Some children ask many questions, and some ask nothing. The kids who ask lots of questions need to be answered, also reassured over and over again. The kids who ask nothing will need to be "coaxed" over the coming months to talk to you, read books with you about it, or draw pictures about it, etc.

Tip #8 Check With Your Kids

Instead of hounding the kids about their feelings, check with them now and then. For example, "Did you talk to anyone?", "Did you find yourself thinking about mom/dad's moving a lot when you're at school?", "How are you doing with the recent changes in our family?", "What did you usually do when you felt sad?". Also, you could suggest the kids talk to a friend, school counselor, dad, mom, sibling, cousin, get a hug from the parent, or punch a pillow and yell when they felt sad.

Kids may keep worrying. Help reassure them that their worries are not realistic and help them think through the idea that life will go on and everything will be okay. Let kids know they can take their favorites toys or other stuffs with them to the new house, their nanny will go back and forth, their pet can go with them, or whatever will make them feel better.

Tip #9 It's Okay For You To Cry Or Choke Up

It's okay to show your sadness and acknowledge that this is a sad family event. However, you will try to help each other to get over it. If one parent begins to say something upsetting or scary for kids or starts to get mad, the other parent should rescue the situation. Try not to make it worse, just say, "Dad/Mom is really upset, and it's hard for all of us. Let's take a break and talk again later." I understand this can be very hard, while for the sake of kids, be forgiving even if your ex-spouse is not handling it well. When kids experience this, they might feel like the world is falling apart, so you need to make the world still feel safe even though the reality as they know it's changing dramatically.

Tip #10 You Will All Get Through It

Let your kids know ALL of you will get through this, and you will. Tell them they will be ok, you will be ok, and you will help each other adapt and adjust to the coming changes. If possible, provide both acceptance and empathy for what your kids feel, and reassure them even the toughest feelings is going to get easier over time. Your openness and positives will make your kids recover and remain open with their feelings with you.

Bonus: Age-by-Age Parental Priorities

- **0 – 5 Years Old**

Parental Priorities: Your consistent nurturing and care will give children a sense of reassurance and stability. Tot's lives need to be anchored by their regular routines, including bed, meals, play, and bath in the presence of the parent who is there for them. This is important since, unlike preteens or teenagers who can escape by going to hand out with friends, but toddlers and preschoolers cannot.

They need concrete and simple explanations. Just stick to the basics: Where they will live, which parent will move out, who is going to look after them and how often they will see the other parent. Provide short answers to their questions, and then wait to see if there are more questions. Do not expect only one conversation to do the job and be ready for several short talks.

6 – 10 Years Old

Parental Priorities: Stable routines and care are still critical. Kids who are at the upper end of this age group can talk about what they are feeling, but they may not want to just because they can. An indirect approach to the topic can help. "Some children feel afraid, sad, or even angry when their parents' divorce," which is less threatening than direct asking, "Are your feeling upset or sad?" Books talking about divorce can also be beneficial.

Age 11 And Up

Parental Priorities: Be open to communication, which will decrease the chance that emotional problems slip under the radar. It can be harder to reach kids at this age. Sometimes they will act as if they don't want to be reached. However, most preteens and teens still need and crave connection with their parents. Some may even test their parents to see if they really cared. So keep talking even though your kids may seem to push you away. Try to make at least some of the conversation about their interested topics or what they would like to talk about.

5. It's Never Too Early To Talk To Kids About Social Media Habits

Whether you like it or not, your kids are probably already obsessing over social medial like Instagram. Even though kids under 13 are not allowed to use social media sites under 13 years old, the number of kids using fake birthdays and creating accounts on popular social media sites using parents' email addresses is kind of startling. The 2017 research from Ofcome, the regulator of the communications service in the UK, has reported that around 28% of 10 years old, 46% of 11 years old, and whopping 51% of 12 years old surveyed has social media profile. Kids are not informed about social media websites or apps from their parents. Instead, they learn from their peers, friends, older siblings, or those influencers. So it's super important that parents take an active role in encouraging the conversations.

As the parent, you should be aware of potential exposure to inappropriate content and cyberbullying. In particular, younger children may not realize their online actions' consequences, which can put them in compromising situations.

Here are tips about how to talk with your kids about appropriate social media habits:

- **Make A Plan**

Start from a place of curiosity and use open-ended questions to help kids identify why they want to join social media like Instagram; what they consider positive experiences on social media would look like for them; who they could turn to if something doesn't go as the planned or make them feel uncomfortable.

This can help them think proactively about how they can define and create positive online experience.

- **Prioritize Privacy**

Many people don't know they are able to be private on Instagram, according to Lori Mahahy, the research lead at Instagram. Making your account on private mode means only approved followers can view, like, and comment on your content, which can help prevent your kids' personal information from ending up in the wrong hands. Let your kids know this and encourage them to set their accounts private and keep an eye on their followers. The rule of thumb is "If you don't know them, don't friend them."

- **Enforce Good Etiquette**

Writing mean comments on social media may get them into trouble, and receiving one can hurt their self-esteem. Talk to your kids about appropriate social media etiquette. Social medial apps like Instagram allow you to filter out inappropriate and offensive words from your comments.

- **Teach Them Accountability**

It's increasingly common for cyberbullying. According to the Centers for Disease Control and Prevention (CDC)'s 2017 Youth Risk Behavior Surveillance System, in the previous 12 months, nearly 15% of surveyed high school students were electronically bullied. It's important to let them know that things that happened online can affect how people feel offline and teach them to take into account with whatever actions they take online. Also, let them know they can remove hateful comments, report negative behaviors, and block individuals.

- **Set Time Limits**

It's not unusual for teens to spend hours on

social media since they are still developing self-discipline. Discuss and decide the proper amount of time they should spend on social media apps every day, whether it's an hour or 20 minutes.

- **Practice What You Preach**

Kids constantly learn by example. By practicing proper social medial habits yourself, you are setting up your kids for an inspiring, positive, and rewarding social media experience.

6. How to Talk To Kids About Bullying

It's a traumatic experience for kids to get bullied. Getting bullied diminishes kids' self-esteem, leaves them feeling anxious and depressed, and can have long-lasting effects. Besides, modern technology nowadays creates more opportunities for bullying than ever before. Unfortunately, all the social networking technology like the Internet and cell phones have opened this whole arena of bullying ways. Cyberbullying is able to reach the victim anywhere, at any time. It can result in profound harm since it can reach a broad audience quickly and leave a permanent footprint online for all involved. Your kids have the right to a nurturing and safe school environment that respects their dignity.

6.1 Help Prevent Bullying

The very first step to keep your kids safe, online or in-person, is making sure they know and understand the issue.

1. **Educate your kids about bullying**. Your kids will be capable of identifying bullying more easily if they know what bullying is, whether it's happening to them or some other students or friends.
2. **Talk frequently and openly to your kids**. The more you talk about bullying with your kids, the more comfortable they will tell you if they experience or see it. If possible, check in with your kids daily and inquire about their time at school and online activities, asking not only about the classes and activities but their feelings.
3. **Help your kids build their confidence**. Encourage kids to join activities they like in your community or enroll in classes they're interested in. This can help them build confidence and a group of good friends who can share interests with.
4. **Help kids be positive role models**. The perpetrator, the victim, and the bystander are the three parties involved in bullying. Even though your ids are not the bullying's victims, they are able to prevent bullying by being respectful, inclusive, and kind to others. If kids witness the bullying, they can also stick up for the victim, question bullying behaviors, and offer support.

5. **Be part of their online experience**. Get to know and familiarize yourself with the platforms you kis are using, explaining how the offline and online worlds are connected. Also warn them about the different risks they are going to face online.
6. **Be the role model**. Treat other adults and children with respect and kindness to show your kids how to behave appropriately, including speaking up when others are being mistreated. Kids usually will look to their parents as examples of how to behave, including what to post online.
7. **Understand The Signs Of Bullying**.

Unless your kid has visible bruises or injuries or tells you about bullying, it's actually difficult for you to know if bullying is happening to your kid.

However, parents can pay attention to the following **warning signs**:

- Not sleeping well, not eating, or not doing the things they enjoyed.
- Seeming anxious or acting differently.
- Avoid certain situations, for example, taking the bus to school or joing school events.

- Seeming more easily upset or moodier than usual.
- Having few friends at school or outside of school.
- Electronics, clothing, or other personal belongs being destroyed or lost.
- Trying to stay close to adults.
- Low academic performance.
- Often asking for money.
- Complaining of stomach aches, headaches, or other physical ailments.
- Getting distressed regularly after spending time on their phone or online without reasonable explanation.
- Behaving secretly, especially when it comes to online activities.

When you suspect the bullying while your kid is reluctant to open up, try to find ways to help them bring up the issue. For example, as you see a situation on a TV show, ask them, "What do you think that person should have done?" or "What do you think of this?" These may lead to questions like, "Have you ever experienced this?" and "Have you ever seen this happen?" You can also try to talk about any experience you or another family had at that age.

6.2 Respond TO Bullying

1. **Forewarn Your Kid**

Be sure they know if something happens, whether online or in school, they should tell you, and you will support them and figure out together how to work it out. If it's happening online, it's very important that they don't respond before telling you about it. It's also vital not to engage with bullying, not feed it by being exactly who the perpetrators look for: someone they can get a rise out of. Let your kids know not to erase those hurtful posts before talking to you. Those should be saved somewhere since you may need to collect evidence of what's been going on sometimes.

2. Listen To Your Kids Calmly And Openly

Focus on making them feel supported and heard, rather than try to solve the problem or find the cause of bullying. Also, make sure they know that it's not their fault.

At the same time, tell your kids that you believe them, you are happy they share with you, and you will do your best to help.

3. Practice Appropriate Responses

Do role-play with your kids at home. Teach them what a couple of lines they can say if bullying happens again. As the kids are humiliated or insulted, they are likely to be stunned, so you want to help make sure they don't react in a way that will add fuel to the fire. Also, teach the following strategies when facing bullies:

- **Don't let the bully make your kids feel bad.**

Teach your kids to say something positive to themselves when someone says something bad about them. Remind themselves of their positive attributes.

- **Don't reward the bully with tears.**

Hurting the feelings is the bully wants. Whining or crying won't work here. Teach your kids to admit the bully is right. For example, when the bully calls your kids "fatty," teach them to look the bully in the eye and just say calmly, "You know, I do need to begin getting more exercise," and then walk away with confidence.

- **Tell the bully how they feel.**

Talk to your kids and let them tell the bully how they feel, why they are feeling it, and what they want the bully to do. Also, teach them do this with a determined and calm voice. For example, "I feel upset when you call me names since I have a real name. I want you to begin calling me by my real name!"

Based on the specific situations, try to come up with several lines for your kids to say and feel comfortable with. Also, it will help to think about friends or other people they can confide in and hope to get support from.

- **Disarm the bully with humor.**

Laugh at the bully's threats and walk away.

- **Teach your kids to use their best judgment and follow the instincts.**

Give your kids an example: if the bully wants your homework and you feel he's going to hurt you. Just give him yours and walk off with confidence. Then report to an adult what have happened.

- **Let your kids not expect to be mistreated.**

Teach your kids to be nice to other kids and do their best to be friendly. The point is to treat others the way they want to be treated. Also, encourage your kids to stand up for other students who are also bullied and ask for a return standing up.

4. **Find Allies**

Encourage your kids to make a deal with their friends: if you stick up for me, I will stick up for you. Data has shown that the most effective way to combat bullying is for the bystander to step in and say, "Hey, this is my friend, don't do that!"

5. Partner With Kid's School Or Teacher

School education can be the best weapon. Research has shown that the most effective way to arm kids against bullying is for schools to begin educating about it, as early as in the first grade. You and your kids don't need to face bullying alone. Reach out to the school for the code of conduct or bullying policy. This can apply both online and in person.

If your kid is being threatened with violence or stalked, you should contact the school as well as the police. In some extreme cases, bullying can evolve into a criminal case, and your top priority is your kids' welfare.

6. Contact the Offender's Parents

This is the right method ONLY for persistent intimidation acts, and you feel those parents will be receptive to working cooperatively with you. Make it clear that your goal is to resolve this together. Email or call them in a nonconfrontational way. You might say something like, “I’m reaching out to you because my daughter came home from school feeling upset every day recently. She told me that John had excluded her from games at the playground and pushed her. I don’t know if John has mentioned any of this at home, but I would like us to help them get along together. Do you have any ideas?”

7. Proven Strategies to Finally Stop Yelling at Your Kids

As Nina Howe, the professor of early and elementary childhood education at Concordia University, mentioned, "Parents yell because something happens that made them feel frustrated and they are getting pulled in a million different directions. They see their kids doing something they don't approve of or the kids are fighting, so they just let loose. It's kind of an automatic response."

If the one universal truth of yelling-as-discipline is that we all do it, the other truth is it's not effective. You are not only making things worse but modeling screaming as a conflict-resolution strategy. Based on a 2013 study, it reported that harsh verbal discipline will not curb problematic behaviors for teens or tweens but will make them more likely to continue doing whatever you are railing against. The study also went far as to compare ongoing and aggressive verbal reprimands with physical disciplines like spanking.

So, is yelling the new spanking? It may be

more socially acceptable to deliver a reprimand trying to get kids' attention. Many of us grew up being yelled at and even spanked. But the final truth is that we don't feel good about ourselves as we launch into a tirade on our next generation. Also, as it frightened us as kids, yelling often frightens our kids, make then anxious, as well as become more prone to yelling themselves.

Kids have sensitive nervous systems, and yelling actually is scary for them since it's intimidating and aggressive. Besides, the facial expressions accompanying yelling are fearful and angry. Even though we get the results we want from yelling, it's because they got scared and just want us to stop. It's not because they really made their own decisions and alter their behaviors. According to experts, what makes yelling insidious is that it may work in the short term, but kids will either learn to turn it out or shut down in the long run.

So as parents, what can we do instead? Let's conquer your yelling habit with the following ten-step program. You have got this!

1. Understand Your Triggers

Yelling is usually a response to specific behavior and doesn't happen just out of the blue, which means something triggers it. So you will have a greater chance to avoid yelling if you can found what causes you to blow a gasket. “It's been a tough day for me at work. I got tired and am coming home, but still have to make dinner. When all the things added up, there may be the chance you are going to lose it.” This kind of self-awareness is going to help you make better choices - for example, you can put on a show to distract the kids as you cook or prepare simple sandwiches for dinner.

2. **Give Kids A Warning**

When your kids fighting in the car or stalling bedtime, it's fair to caution them that you are about to get shouty. Say something like, “You are pushing me, and I don't want to yell just to get your attention. But if you still don't listen, I might lose it.” This kind of sober warning can sometimes be enough to get your kids to tone it down.

You are allowing your kids to prepare mentally for a transition by giving them a warning. Perhaps they didn't respond to your repeated pajamas directives because they are engrossed in a book or their toys. Give them a heads-up. “It's time to go to bed. Do you need ten more minutes? I think I can handle ten more minutes, but then time is up."

3. Take A Time Up

Judy Arnall, a child development specialist, recommends a calm-down strategy is to go into the bathroom, and yell into the toilet and flush it away. This is considered as an equivalent of taking a time out: leaving the room physically and then having a strategy to compose yourself, whether it involves sending in your spouse to deal or squeezing a stress ball. It really can help us practice better self-control if we can commit to mindfully changing our behavior and taking just a few minutes out before we do anything.

4. Make A Yes List

Understandably, taking an adult time out is easier said than done. That's why it will help for families to sit down together and create your Yes list that can be taped to the fridge. The Yes List is to list the acceptable things to do before you say something or scream that you are going to regret. This list varies from family to family, while it could include actions like winging the Chuckit ball for the dog or jogging in place. It's beneficial if parents have a plan in place. If you do things on your Yes List, such as take a deep breath or go to the bathroom, your kids are watching these too and probably will pick up on these things and do them as well.

5. Understand What Is Considered Normal Behavior

It's helpful to know that your kids' whining, sibling rivalry, bedtime aversion, and mouthiness are age-appropriate and normal, which can also make the actions less personal. What made us yell is the idea that the kids shouldn't have done something, that there's something wrong with the kids and the yourselves. If you remove that, then it can become something to deal with.

6. Teach The Lesson Later

Yelling or shouting is not communicating, and it will encourage your kids to shut down instead of listening and actually will undermine the legitimacy of parents' concerns. You might feel the anger parachuting in, and it can be hard to wait. However, exercising self-control in the moment is going to deliver a stronger message overall. Actually, it's way more effective as you are calmer. The teaching moment can come later, as with oxygen masks on an airplane, and you need to calm first. Once you calm down, you will be able to talk it out, explain your expectations of their behaviors and the consequences with younger kids. Your son was being sassy? Ask how his day was, and explain how his words made you feel. Your daughter made a mess? Clean it up together.

7. Being Proactive

Some experts also call this the "strike while the iron's cold" parenting approach. For example, if getting out of the house always could escalate into a shouting match in the morning, prep the night before. Send your kids to bed wearing socks so you won't have to nag and nag, then yell about socks in the morning. It can make a huge difference by applying this simple shift.

Some other examples include: When you are running errands, pack activities to keep your kids busy and get them less likely to fight with each other; Bring snacks to head off mid-hike whining, etc.

8. Realize When It's Not Your Kids' Misbehaviors. It's About You.

Yelling is often not just about a misbehaving kid, and it can be an outward manifestation of your own unmet needs. Self-reflection and meditation are likely to help. Ask yourself, "What's going on for me to yell at my kids for the past three days in a row? Do I feel unappreciated? Did I not sleep enough? What else is going on for me apart from my kids' behaviors."

9. Adjust Your Expectations

It's vital to keep your expectations with kids realistic. Part of the reason we yell is that reality doesn't meet our high hopes. This advice applies to simpler scenarios as well. Run fewer errands, give one directive at a time, plan a shorter hike. Or abandon your expectations altogether, such as it's no shame in ditching a full grocery cart in an aisle.

10. Have A Yelling Debrief

What if you lose it. You were not prepared. What to do now? Apologize is the right choice. It is like taking the sting out of an ugly situation. It reminds our children that we are human, and sometimes emotions lead us to speak or behave in ways we are not proud of.

The saying sorry model appropriates behavior for kids to follow if they lose their temper. It can help them cement the between the resulting yelling and the big emotion. Also, talk about what prompts the yelling since it's usually not just about the parent losing control but also about the kid needing to alter their behaviors—this requires a team approach. If some behaviors in your kids are irritating or other things have set you off, talk about it and discover a way to solve it so it won't happen so often. This can be a win-win: yell less, and you will find you have fewer reasons to get shouty soon.

Any Time Is Okay To Yell?

Besides the apparent scenarios, including cheering kids at a soccer game, yelling out of excitement or happiness like "Happy New Year!" Experts agree that sometimes it is ok to "yell" to get your kids' attention as they might in danger. You want to save those yells for the times when you really need them to listen, such as they are not stopping at the end of the sidewalk. This is also why you won't want to reply on yelling continuously, because it does sometimes work, but it won't work if you use it all the time.

Section 4

Get Your Kids To Talk To You

– Age-By-Age Guide

It turns out that connections kids need to feel with their parents in order to talk to them and open up is cemented long even before their teen stage. A parenting coach at Vancouver, Julie Romanowski, says that your children's communication skills are built in toddlerhood, even in infancy. In your little one's infancy stage, as your baby cried and you picked your baby up, you were showing you are someone he/she can trust or count on. Even though it's not so straightforward being that trusted confidante, as your children's everyday life experience grows to include other things like friendships, bullying, academic pressure, and other social issues, it's still vital that we can maintain that bond helping our kids process and sort through the things that happen to them. You might not hear about their every single trial and triumph, but these ideas could get your children to open up to you at every age.

We don't have to be our kids' best friends. However, something more than a grunt as we ask about their day would be nice, surely.

Now, here's how to kick-start the conversations with your kids.

- **Preschoolers**

Are you familiar with this classic scenario: as you pick up your child from preschool or daycare and ask what she did in the day, and what you got is "Nothing" or "I don't know." You might feel your child didn't want to share with you and had no idea how to continue the conversation.

While this is because although preschoolers can understand a lot, they are still developing the needed language skills to express what they would like to say. Honestly, it requires a lot of work to explain how your day went, as you have to synthesize and funnel all that information and organize it into concise sentences that are going to make daddy or mommy happy. As a result, it's much easier for your little one just to say "I don't know."

In order to help your kid zero in on a detail or an anecdote, try to ask more specific questions and include a prompt. For example, "What did you like better today, the circle time or snack time?" If you are more familiar with your children's daily schedule, your questions can be even more specific. If you are not, some relatively general question may help,"Did you sing any song today?" or "Who did you play with today?"

Instead of these details, if you want to know how your child is feeling today, you can observe his/her behavior and then ask about it. You could say something like, "You had a bit of a funny face when I picked you up. What happened?"

Once your child did mention something negative from his/her day, of course, you should show your concern but make sure that you don't overact. If your reactions are too much, children are very likely to shut down. The child may have a fine day, but one thing happened, making them upset. If you show the alarm sign on your face, your child may also stop sharing this kind of information since they think it probably would only make you too upset. So as the parent, empathize with your children, let them know how crummy it must have felt to have his toy grabbed from him, and then move on.

- **Little Kids**

It's not smart to begin an interrogation as soon as you arrive for pickup or the moment you both walk in the front door. This may even be a mistake for some children. Imagine you picked up your children and ask about 20 questions. This probably is the last thing they want after being "on" all day at school already.

You can just spend a few minutes reconnecting with your children by being present. Consider saying something simple like, "I missed you. Let me help you with your backpack." Then you child may think: My mom/dad got my back. This is when they are going to begin opening up.

If you are working full-time and cannot see your kids until 6 p.m., or if you are shuttling your kid from school to another activity like going home for dinner, you might find it a little hard to fit in a few minutes to connect. At this time, you can work some parent-kid time into your day, such as after dinner. Sit down to do a focused activity together, for example, 10 minutes of puzzle or coloring. This will create that space where your children start to feel like talking since you gave them the message that you are available for them. Besides, you can take advantage of regular moments you can have together, such as walking to school in the morning, car rides, low-pressure chats, and bedtime for casual. Start with sharing a few details from your own day to encourage the conversation, and it should not feel like the one-side interrogation. Your kids will also learn that everyone has good and bad days, no matter how old you are.

Susan found that keeping in the loop about who her grade-three daughter is playing with or the curriculum helped her bring things up in conversation. If she wants to dig deeper into what's happening in her daughter's life, she chooses to use their shared journal where Susan writes down questions and her daughter could think about and answer when she has time. The questions Susan likes to ask including "What do you wish as different?" or "What made you feel the happiest when you were at school today?", she will ask her daughter to write her back. If she feels their communication has stalled, Susan will use her daughter's responses as the springboard for more conversations.

Also, remember if you brush off or ignore your child when a guest speaker came into his classroom on that day, or he is rattling on about the latest video game, you probably are missing a chance to show you are a good listener. Your phone is put down, and your body is leaning if you are really connected. You can find that your children will come to you for the complicated stuff If you do a really nice job in these moments.

Big Kids

Your kids getting older is inevitable, and you won't be present physically in every aspect of their lives. However, you are still needed for emotional support. At this stage, if you want a window into their days, the key is to focus less on solutions or results but to keep up the listening (may as hard as it might be). If your child is having an issue with a friend, you may be tempted to suggest he find other people to hang out with. As parents, we tend to be the problem-solvers, but as soon as we begin problem-solving, the judgments come too. However, people don't want to be judged.

Actually, the car is an excellent place to talk

with the kids at this age since they don't need to make eye contact with you. Some kids may feel uncomfortable with making contact with their parents. Carving out a special one-on-one time at least once a month is another great idea, for example, watching a favorite TV show together. This will let you get some quality time and share an interest.

Also, pay attention to your kids' body language. Whether it's with words, tears, or shrugs, or even looking away as they see you, they are always talking to you. Consider saying something like, "I love you, and I can see something has happened from your body language, and you are not ready to tell me. Whenever you are ready, I'm here."

If your teens do open up and talk to you, make sure to stay neutral, especially they tend to be fairly closed off with their feelings. While if you begin looking panic, they will think: this is worse than I thought. So it's crucial to use that neutral, calm, and constant voice.

Your ultimate goal is wanting your kids to enjoy talking with you. Whether they are telling something they are scared about or something fun, the more they feel better from any interaction, the more likely they are going to come back. This is your only hope for finding out more about what's happening in their lives.

Section 5

How To Resolve Conflicts Effectively

1. Parent-Child Conflicts

1.1 Why Do Parents and Kids Get Into Conflicts?

Any close relationships will experience some conflicts, especially when they happen between the parent and the kid. Conflicts occur when two individuals don't agree based on their values, beliefs, or goals. They are not always as simple as arguments and usually happen right before the arguments.

Especially for the adolescent stage, it's a time when parental influence and independence clash, since teens can think independently but still need to live with their parents who have expectations and rules for them. As kids grow up, they are getting different values and beliefs from their parents.

The hottest topics for parent-child conflicts include:

- Curfew
- Cell phone use
- Noises (whether it's party, the TV or an electric guitar)
- Boyfriend/Girlfriend
- Religion/Church
- Grades
- Fairness
- Personal Appearance
- Dishonesty
- Using hot water/electricity

1.2 Three Common Parent-Child Conflict Types and Some Helpful Remedies

1. Boundary Conflict

This conflict happens when parents try to set limits with their kids. Although limits are a vital part of creating the structure for kids, setting limits will create tension between kids and parents, leading to the emotional relationship disconnect.

To keep connected during these limit-setting interactions, the key is aligning yourself with kids' primary emotional states. Empathize and reflect on kids' desires without actually fulfilling their wishes. For instance, rather than simply say, "No, you cannot go outside," say, "I know you want to go outside, but it's also important that you finish your homework first, and then you can play outside for a while."

Allowing your kids have their distress without trying to punish them will provide the opportunity to learn how to tolerate their own emotional discomfort. As the parent, you do not have to fix the situation by giving in or removing uncomfortable emotions. Letting your kids have their feelings and letting them know that you understand it can be hard not to get what they want is the most helpful and kindest thing you can do for your kids at the moment. Your kids will learn to regulate their emotions during the process too.

2. Inevitable Conflict

This is the periodic conflict that we cannot avoid in all of our close relationships. It's inevitable because we cannot always be mindful, sensitive, and attentive to those close to us. Sometimes we will show impatience, overreact, miss verbal or non-verbal cues, etc. As kids feel disconnected in these scenarios, they will have a heightened need to be understood.

3. Intense Conflict

This one involves intense emotional distress and causes a significant disconnection between the parent and the kid. It happens when the parents lose control of their emotions and begin name-calling, screaming, or threatening toward the kid. Since this conflict accompanying a sense of shame, it's the most distressing kind of disconnections for kids.

Both parents and kids feel the overwhelming feeling of shame. The parents can feel a deep sense of inadequacy which may be triggered by feeling incompetent or helpless. The kid feels shame from being demeaned, criticized, or ridiculed.

1.3 How to Reduce Parent-Child Conflicts

1. Making Eye Contact

Kids Sometimes are not listening when the parent speaks to them. They can be engrossed in a game, or their eyes are glued to the TV. Usually, parents respond by yelling or getting upset.

Instead of forcibly making kids tune out of the

noise, you can walk over to your children, be on eye level with them, make eye contact, and then begin to speak to them.

Please note if you have never tried this before, there's a chance that your kid may challenge you. What you need to do is to keep your cool and provide them clear directives.

2. Offering Choices

When kids are not listening to your directives, offer two choices to them. A choice will make your kids feel valued and keep them from feeling as if they are stuck with their parents' decisions.

For instance, your son won't stop playing the game at dinner time, and you can say, "Dane, you can choose to play for two more minutes and come to eat dinner. Or you can choose to have me turn off the video game in 2 minutes, and you cannot play the game tomorrow. "

By providing options to your kids, you teach them responsibilities and give them the feeling of having control.

3. A-C-T

Use this technique when you find your kids doing something they are not supposed to do:

- A- Acknowledge the feelings. Simply use one sentence to let kids know you understand their feelings or desires. Such as, "Mike, I know you want to go to the park and play with your friends…"
- C- Communicate the Limit. Make them know the limit to their behaviors (not their feelings).
  Such as, "But you need to finish your homework first."
- T- Target alternatives. Offer them an alternative behavior, so they will not need to fixate on the inappropriate one. Such as, "You can watch some TV after you finish the homework."

The alternative behavior should also allow them to feel they still can have some fun. Validate kids while let them know there are healthy limits when applying this technique.

4. Setting Clear Consequence

If your kids are still not listening after you tried the A-C-T technique, you can follow a related and natural consequence to their behaviors. For example, if your son cannot use the dart gun appropriately or responsibly, he will lose the privilege of playing it.

Setting a consequence can place the responsibilities on kids to make the appropriate choice of behaviors, rather than let them feel you punish them.

5. Creating A Routine

This usually will make kids feel secure and safe because they know what's going to come next. Most kids thrive on routines.

When kids are at school, the school's routines help them go through their day in an organized way. After they come back home, they can relax, but it doesn't mean they don't need a routine. They can have some free time at home. However, let them know they have enjoyed the relaxing time and need to follow the homework time.

If your child is too young to tell the time, try the timer and give them time to transition from free time to homework time. Also, talk to other parents and learn about the routines that have worked for their kids.

Following these tips can help reduce the conflicts with your kids and improve your relationship. This probably is not easy at the beginning, but if you keep at it, it will become easier with time.

1.4 Positive Strategies for Solving Conflicts, Back Talk, and Arguments

Do you dislike conflicts while feeling like whenever you set a limit, the conflict is inevitable?

Conflicts can be disappointing, difficult, annoying, and exasperating, and it is also a disconnect to argue and engage in those power struggles. Let's look at the more positive ways that handle family conflicts and lead to actual resolutions.

1. **Listen with the intent to understand.**

For example, when your child is trying to argue with you about getting a new toy, there is a great place to listen, stop the conflict, and understand.

- "Hmm… I see it very important to you."
- "So this toy is your favorite? I heard you. It looks fun to play with."

2. **Stay positive.**

Avoid using a reactive attitude to approach a conflict and with the intent to have the final say. Instead, aim to understand, resolve, and respond.

3. **Instead of control, focus on cooperation.**

It will help resolve a conflict when BOTH sides can discuss and give input about the situation.

- "You can let me know what you are thinking, and I'll share mine too. We can find a solution together."
- "What would you propose we do about this?"
- "We will both have a chance to talk, while let's take turns so that we can really listen to each other."
- "I would like to share my reasons and then listen to yours."

4. **Ask open questions (especially effective for older children)**

- "What about…?"
- "Can you share more of your thoughts?"
- "Why do you think that?"

5. **Provide choices (particularly helpful with younger ones)**

- "I know you want the black pants, but they are washing. So how about the blue ones or the jeans you choose."

- “Which toy would you like to put away first, the puzzle into the drawer or the truck into the toy box?”
- “I heard that you like the cake and want another piece, but you had a lot already today. What time will you want to have the cake tomorrow, after lunch or morning snack?”

6. Ask for reasons.

Learning how to argue their points of view respectfully during conflict resolution is a must-learned step for kids. Practice it with your kids now.

- “Could you please explain why this is important to you?”
- “Can you give me three solid reasons to support your thinking?”
- “These are my reasons to say No. Can you turn them around with your own reasons?”
- “I want to hear more about your idea. What else you could share?”

7. Strike a deal.

Allow your kids to propose a different solution, or you offer a deal. However, it’s not the same as giving in or letting them rule the house. Striking an agreement means the solution will work for everyone.

- "This way doesn't work, but any other ways you can think of?"
- "I can't agree to the sleepover on Monday night, but if you can propose another date, we can discuss it."
- "If you stop by grandma to wish her a Happy Birthday first, then I will agree you go over to your friend's house for the rest of the time of the day. Deal?"

8. Model flexibility.

It's not about giving in if you say YES to your children when they give you some good reasons. This represents flexibility.

"I hear your reasons, and you have convinced me. I appreciate we all could stay cool about this, so YES!"

"You know what, I'm impressed that you have thought this through, so I'll say YES this time."

9. It's beneficial to rewind.

Sometimes, it's also ok to pause and rewind.

- "We seem to argue instead of talking about this. Let's start over."

- "Arguing won't get us anywhere. Let's take a break, and try again after we cool off."
- "Ooops, we are arguing, and it's getting nowhere. Let's try again."

10. Hold family meetings.

Set a time every week or month when everyone can practice making requests and discuss issues peacefully, like asking mom for the ride to a friend's house, etc.

11. Delay the discussion.

We can delay the argument and return to it to resolve it when everyone is ready to argue respectfully.

- "I understand how much you want this, but it's not the right place/right time. Let's talk about it when we arrive home."
- "I would like to talk about this when you are able to do it respectfully."
- "I'd like to talk about this when we are cooled off. I will be in the kitchen, come and find me when you are ready."
- "Let's put this on hold until later when I'm ready to listen to you."

12. Aim to set limits with firmness, respect, and kindness in mind.

Sometimes, we need to say no and set a limit, but we can do it positively.

- "I know how much you like this while my answer is NO."
- "This is delicious. Although you want more tonight, it's not the time for you to have anymore."
- "I know you like this toy. Let's put it on your wish list. Today is not the day we buy it."
- "I've made my decision. I need to keep you safe, and my final answer will be no. "

13. Support the disappointment.

What if you've set the limit, but your child doesn't like it and responds with whining, crying, and yelling? Support them in the disappointment.

Avoid belittling the situation using comments like "It's not a big deal, stop crying." Or "don't be ridiculous." Your child needs time to process the disappointment. Be nearby to support them and have faith in them that they will be able to overcome or handle their feelings.

14. Strengthen your connection.

You may feel like most of your time spent with your kids in conflicts, and you will find the biggest change coming from spending time together to connect. You may also want to reflect on how you can approach the communication with your children or decide if there is anything you can do about your own attitude. Are you demanding or commanding a lot from your child? Or are you involving your child and inviting cooperation?

Conflicts can serve an excellent purpose to learn to listen and trust each other, as well as bring you closer. They can also help your child grow capable of problem-solving, and handling disappointment and frustration.

1.5 Facilitating Repair After Conflicts

Conflicts can cause an overwhelming feeling of shame in both parents and children. The parent will feel a deep sense of inadequacy triggered by feeling incompetent or helpless. The child can feel the same from being demeaned, criticized, or ridiculed. Repairing this will be super beneficial to your parent-child relationship after conflicts. So how to facilitate the repair?

Repair is an interactive experience usually starting with the parent's own centering process. If the parents are still resentful or angry toward their child, it is generally impossible for the true emotional repair to happen. Besides, children pick up that the parent is not fully emotionally available intuitively and will respond cautiously.

First step: Be aware of your own emotion.

You will have a hard time allowing your children to express their emotions fully if you are comfortable with your emotion.

Some questions that you can consider:

- Are you explosive when you express you anger? If you are, what may be the source of that behavior?
- Are there emotions that you are not comfortable expressing (sadness, guilt, anger, anxiety)?
- Did you overreact to situations that seem out of your control?

The anger you feel might block you from seeing your child's need for reconnection and keeping you from making efforts at repairing. Being able to focus on your experience and that of your child is a central feature of effective repair.

Second step: Initiate repair with your

children.

Respect and learn your child's style for reconnecting and processing. It is the parent's role to initiate the repair. Start by addressing the disconnection neutrally.

For instance, you can say, "This has been difficult for both of us to fight like this. I would like us to feel good about each other again. Let's talk about it." If your first few attempts meet with a dismissive attitude, don't give up.

To start the repair process, you need to resist the urge to blame. As the parent, you are responsible for knowing your internal emotional issues and your own behaviors.

Do not need to dismiss or conceal the emotional moments with your children. Otherwise, your child will learn this too. You permit your children to express themselves by taking the lead. By appropriately expressing your emotions, you are teaching them that strong emotions can be expressed and managed.

Third step: Listen carefully to your children's feelings and thoughts.

Allow and encourage your child to express how

the conflict experience felt to them. As long as it's done respectfully and won't create unsafe situations, let them express the emotions fully.

Do not counter or judge their expression. Also, do not defend yourself. You can share your experience of the interaction after they fully express themselves. Take the interaction as the teaching opportunity to set boundaries on how to express strong emotions. Join your children emotionally by reflecting on what you heard from them.

The way we communicate with the children shapes how they learn to regulate their impulses and emotions.

1.6 When to seek professional help

* If you and your kids continue to struggle, feel free to contact a child counselor or family therapist for support

* Call 911 anytime if you think your kids or you may need emergency care:

- You are afraid your kids might hurt you or someone else;
- You are so frustrated with your kids that you are afraid you might hurt them.

* Watch closed for your kids' behavioral changes and make sure to contact your doctors if:

  - You want to see a behavior counselor.
  - You want suggestions to help your kids control their behaviors.

2. Friendship Conflicts

Having a best friend is one of life's greatest joys. However, what do you do when your children run into problems with their friends? Maybe your child found out on social media that his friends are having fun without inviting him. Or he didn't get invited to a birthday party. Some friends may stop talking to each other for a while. Your child may think this means his friendship is over when this happens, which can be devastating.

It is one of the most important life lessons children can learn to work out troubles. If they can handle it well, they will be able to keep the friendships instead of losing them. Some kids can deal with these easily, while others struggle. As the parent, you play an important role in teaching kids how to work out friendship problems positively.

Helping Children Work It Out

Validating your children's feelings is one of the first vital ways to help them deal with friendship conflicts.

Just keep it simple, “I’m really sorry to hear that you are having trouble with your friend. I understand it’s really tough. Would you like to talk about it?” which is much better than just telling the kid that they will work it out or it’s nothing to be upset – these will invalidate their feelings and minimize their friendship’s importance. Share your similar experiences letting your kids know that you understand what they are suffering and what it’s like to have fights with close friends.

Get your children to talk more about the conflict by asking questions. Here are some examples to try:

- Have you both talked about it?
- Why do you think that happened?
- What do you think your friend is feeling?
- How do you feel about it?
- What do you think you could do to work it out?

If you would like to offer advice, ask your child first. It’s a respectful approach to ask, “Would you like to hear some ideas on how to handle this?” which will make it more likely that your child will be open to your advice. Also, let your child know it will be his decision on how to deal with this situation in the end.

If your children are open to advice, suggest they figure out what caused the problems. Talking to the friend directly will be the best way. If your child's feeling got hurt, but it's just a one-time upsetting thing, he might choose to let it go. However, if it's something that repeatedly happened, for example, a friend never returning texts or phone calls or never being invited to parties, your child will need to talk about it with his friend. It can hurt friendships or cause other issues if he just holds on to those bad feelings and does not share. What's worse is that your child takes out his anger in other unwanted ways.

Trying to solve problems by text or over the phone won't go well. Encourage your child to talk face-to-face. It's challenging to figure out other people's feelings when you cannot see them talking to you. Also, remind your children not to send an angry text or message, since once they sent it, it cannot be taken back. Here is an example you can share with your child, "Justin, can I talk to you about something important? I felt terrible about our argument the other day. How did you feel about it?"

If you think that your child may have behaved in the way that contributed to the conflict, or your child might not be telling the entire story, consider talking to the friend's parents, especially you know them well. If both kids are willing, you might be able to work together to solve the problem. Kids need an opportunity to work it out independently, so don't jump into the solution first. If the conflict problem involves friends from school, consider suggesting your child talk to the school counselor about the issue. The school counselor may provide to meet both kids to help me figure out this problem.

There is an exception to "let kids work it out independently" is bullying. Experts agree that adults need to get involved with this unhealthy issue.

Model And Encourage Forgiving And Apologizing.

Even for adults, admitting we are wrong is hard. While it's still the quickest way to solve the disagreements and get back to friendship. One way for your child to forgive and apologize easier is for you to model it in your daily lives. If your children observe you apologizing when you say something hurtful or overreact, it will be easier for them to do the same with their friends.

Help your children understand that apologizing

can help the other person feel better quicker, even if they didn't mean to be hurtful. Let the child know that keeping it simple will work best, "I can understand why you're upset. I'm really sorry that I hurt your feelings. I should have dealt with that better."

It only makes things worse between friends if holding a grudge. Forgiving is also the key.

When To Consider Seeking Professional Help

Some children have more social skill problems. For instance, kids with mental disorders can have more trouble empathizing with others, controlling their impulses, noticing others are upset with them, or handling conflicts. Consider counseling when these problems interfere with the child's ability to get along with others.

Section 6

Love Languages of Kids

1. What Are the Love Languages of Kids

Did you try to give your children a huge bear hug when you collect them from school, but only for them to wriggle away with a frown? Or have you handed your teenager a gift which you spent hours choosing, only for them to thank you while not seem to give it much more though particularly? If you have more than one kid, you might notice that what means a lot to one may have little impact on another. It can be very confusing when your kids don't respond to your love gestures as you expected.

So what's going on? It may be that your kids have different "love languages." We have realized that every kid is different, but what is probably not so obvious is that how one kid communicates love could not be received in the same way by another.

Dr.Gary Chapman introduced the Love languages concept. Chapman suggests that children, as well as adults, receive and express love in five major different ways. We all have a primary love language that we use to communicate love best to us.

Once you know your kid's love language, you can improve the relationship between you and connect with your kids on a deeper level that means more to them. The primary point of understanding and applying love languages is to fill each other's love tank. By doing the things filling out your kids' love tank in their specific ways, you are sending them a message clear and loud- you are loved.

If you observe your kids over time, their love languages will become clear. After you get to know your kids' love languages, enjoy the fun of delivering the love messages to them in a way that can fill their love tanks to the top.

Love Language: Physical Touch

Do you have a kid who:

- Loves to cuddle, snuggle, and be close;
- Asks to sit on your top;
- Often leans on you, grabs your hand to hold it, or affectionately rubs you;
- Never seems to leave your side.

Your kid's love language may be **Physical Touch**.

If your kids keep appearing in your space, playing with your hair, or touching you, that's a signal that they would like to be touched more.

Kisses and hugs are the most common way of speaking this type of love language, while there are other ways as well. A mom reads the story with her four-year-old on her lap. A dad spins his son in the air and laugh happily together. For them, physical touch communicate love much deeper than the words do.

Some research has proved that lack of parental love and warmth will make children get stressed since parents sometimes don't balance the pressure put on them to succeed with affection.

Love Language: Words of Affirmation

Do you have a kid who:

- Is highly motivated by your encouraging words;
- Likes to hear you retell stories about them and relish your storytelling;
- Says the sweet affirmations, such as "I love you so much, mommy" or "You're the best daddy.";
- Will get lighted up when you give positive feedback or praises;

Your kid's love language may be **Words of Affirmation**.

Words can be powerful in communicating love. Praises, compliments, and speaking highly of them are like the fuel to their soul. They love hearing all the things you love about them and tend to feed off others' validation. Words like "I care about you." are like a warm and gentle rain falling on their souls, nurturing the kids' inner sense of security and worth. They will not be forgotten soon even though such words are quickly said. This groups of kids can reap the affirming words' benefits for a lifetime.

At the same time, they can be more affected by harsh discipline or verbal correction.

Love Language: Quality Time

Do you have a kid who:

- Always try to seek your attention to be with them one-on-one or watch them;
- Asks you to play with them or spend time with them;
- Wants to get your attention and says things like, “let me show you something.” or “watch this.”
- They will look to see what you are doing every time you turn around.

Quality time also refers to focused attention. For the kids whose love language is quality time, they want your undivided attention. If they didn’t get the attention they seek, they would try to get attention somewhere else. This is also where they can get those negative attentions.

The point is, they want to be with you. You can fill their love bucket by spending at least 10 mins with them every day. Quality time is the parents’ gift of presence to the kids. You are conveying the message:” I like being with you. You’re important.” The quality time can let the kids feel that they are the most important person in the world to the parents.

You need to go to their emotional/physical development level. For example, riding bikes, playing a game after school, or lying in bed talking before they drift off to sleep. The key factor here is not the activities themselves, but you are being together and doing something together.

If your kids' primary love language is quality time, your kids will experience a gnawing uneasiness without sufficient quality time. They may consider their parents do not really love them.

Love Language: Gifts

Do you have a kid who:

- Remembers gifts they received years ago;
- Cherishes gifts;
- Looks happy and loved when they receive gifts;
- Takes time unwrapping gifts;

Your kids' love language may be **Gifts**;

Receiving and giving gifts can be a powerful love expression, which can extend into later years. The gifts that truly convey love are part of love languages, and the most meaningful gifts can become the symbol of love.

For kids whose primary love language is gifts, they see receiving gifts as a special moment and value the same packaging as the actual gift. You might be surprised to find they can remember each gift they have received, how it's wrapped, even after months or years after receiving it.

You may also notice your kid loves collecting the gifts and has trouble throwing them out over the years, even if it's with missing pieces, broken, or hasn't been played for years.

They usually don't see gifts as material objects but as the symbol representing your love for them.

Love Language: Acts of Service

Do you have a kid who:

- They look for things that need to be done, such as putting back the toys left in the corner. This will let them feel accomplished and proud, so showing your appreciation can go a long way;

- Your child naturally look for ways to help others and will even actively doing things like putting away disease or folding the laundry;

Or

- Begs you to help me, like making their bed, or fix a toy, etc.;
- Asks you to do things for them even though they can do it themselves or know how to do it.
- Says things like," can't you do it?" or "you do it for me."

Your kid's love language may be **Acts of Service.**

They can either very actively help you do something. However, you can also feel like a servant to your kids. Because their love language is acts of service, they will feel your love when you do things for them. When your kid asks you to fix a toy, he or she not just want to get the task done. Your kid is crying for emotional love.

Since it's good for your child to be self-reliant, you don't need to jump at every one of their requests. But your occasional acts of service mean a lot to them. It also means that you need to be sensitive to those requests and understand that your response should fill the kids' love tank or else puncture the tank. Every one of their requests calls for a loving, thoughtful response.

Now it's time to identify your kid's primary love language.

2. How to connect your kids using love languages

2.1 Connect With Your Child Using Love Languages

Now we know kids express and experience love differently. Before we get started, let's talk more how to identify your kids' primary love language.

The best way to identify is by paying attention to what your kids ask of you and how they show you love. We all tend to give affection in the way we prefer to receive it. After we grow up, we learn that we need to offer love to others in a way that works for them. While kids usually don't pick up on that, they provide the type of affection they crave.

For example, if your daughter likes to ask to cuddle on the couch, snuggle several extra minutes before bed, or hold your hands when you talk outside together. You can figure out her primary love language is physical contact, and it is how she feels most connected with the mom and dad.

Having different love languages within a family

can happen, so sometimes it can be tricky to navigate. But once you learn your kids' love language, it will make all the differences not only in their happiness but your relationship.

 # Physical Touch

If your kid's primary love language is physical touch, which means physical touch communicates love to them more deeply than those encouragements, fixing the toy, or buying gifts. Their love tanks will remain unfill without pats on the back, kisses, or other physical expressions of love.

Express Love to Your Kid by:

- Playing games like Pat-a-Cake, twister, piggy-back or on-the-shoulder rides, etc.
- For smaller children, giving lots of hugs, kisses, offering them to sit on your lap.
- For older children, holding hands, high-five, patting on the back, or an arm around their shoulder.
- Squeeze their hands gently and say, "I love you!"
- Read a book or watch their favorite TV shows snuggled up on the couch.
- Create a special and fun kind of handshake or a silent signal between

you. For example, squeezing their hands twice means “I love you.”

- Challenge them to a thumb- or an arm-wrestling contest.
- Morning and evening hugs or kisses.
- Wake them up with a warm snuggle sweetly, rather than light on and a “wake up!”
- Do stretches or yoga together using each other for gentle support and resistance.
- When they are upset, ask your kid if you want a hug or need affection.

Common Pitfalls:

To any kid, a spanking or slap is hurtful, but it can be devastating to those whose love language is physical touch. According to the research, dads tend to be less physically affectionate as their daughters begin to develop. While making a habit of good-morning or good-night hugs are still beneficial.

 # Words of Affirmation

These children feel loved by words. Telling them how much you appreciate them or how great they did can mean the whole world to them. On the other hand, they may take negative comments very hard.

Express Love to Your Kid by:

- Write your kid a love note in the lunch box or around the house.
- Say, "I love you." to them several times every day.
- Look them in the eye and tell them how important they mean to you.
- Use encouraging phrases or words often.
- Send them a text message letting them know how awesome they are. Need to be genuine and specific.
- Affirm both their achievements and efforts.
- Reinforce their love language by praising the characteristics and qualities you love most about them.
- Create a name of affection for your kid that is called only between you.
- Always be ready to say something awesome to them when they are with their siblings or friends.
- Tell them you love them without a "...but" following your affection words. Otherwise, they will think your love is conditional.
- Get them a nice journal and write inspiring messages on the first page, and date it. Journaling is often a great encouraging activity for these kids.

- Allow your kids to overhear you speaking brightly about them to families or friends.
- Offer very specific praise, such as, "It's so awesome when you did…"
- Create a fan sign for your kids at their events, like their sports games. Also, if appropriate, scream their name loudly.
- Always reserve discipline or correction to be given privately within your home and not in front of others. Also can try the sandwich method. Praise-correction-praise.
- When they make mistakes, acknowledge their good determinations intentions, or efforts, etc.

Common Pitfalls:

For these kids, insults cut deep. Avoid those phrases that imply conditional love "I love you, but…" or "I love you when…"

 # Quality Time

These children feel loved as you put down what you are doing and provide them with your undivided attention. They crave time with you above all else and can be keenly aware if you are not fully present with them.

Express Love to Your Kid by:

- Bring your kids together during errands or allow them to help you around the house.
- Find silly things to do and laugh about together.
- Stop the things you are doing and make eye contact with your kids when telling and sharing something.
- Have a regularly special time for your kid and listen to their feelings and stories.
- Play with your children or do fun activities together. Learn what they love to play and try to make those games more fun. You can also find many engaging activities and games for all family members.
- Create a family project that the whole family can enjoy when it's finished.
- If possible, pause what you are doing for ten minutes when your kids ask you to watch them or play with them.
- Take up some physical activities together, such as running. You can train and run marathons together throughout the year.
- Identify a hobby, a sport, or their talent and try to get involved. For example, be a volunteer or a coach, and start your own group.

- Cook a meal together. Also, let them do the planning, help with shopping, and prepare it.
- Provide your kids your presence. Don't have to be the running conversations. It may be enough to simply sit next to them and do your reading as they are doing their homework.
- Rearrange or reorganize a room together.

Common Pitfalls:

If your kids' primary love language is quality time, don't send them back to the room or isolate them for a time-out since these will be severe punishment to them. You also don't need to assume that spending extra time together means that you have to abandon your to-do list. Simple company will let them feel your warm presence, and you can do your work or reading when they are absorbed in their own play.

 # Gifts

The kids how often give you something small, such as flowers from the garden, prefer to feel loved through gifts. Those presents also can be provided together with other love languages. But there is a difference between kids who beg and whine for a toy when you're shopping every time and those who consider gifts as your love extension. The kids whose primary love language is gifts will be happy with the smallest presents, even handmade ones.

Express Love to Your Kid by:

- Choose thoughtful, small, and inexpensive or homemade gifts. This can mean a lot to your kids during both special occasions and ordinary days.
- Gift your kid a song, either a special song that reminds you of them or the one you create.
- Buy your kid a special shirt capturing their personality.
- Create a photo album about them with some special moments you've shared and/or they are doing something they love.
- Keep some stickers or charts to record their achievements and rewarding kids with small gifts.
- Make a collection of wrapping paper with their favorite colors and unique gift boxes which can be used for the simplest presents.

- Consider meaningful and unique gifts like planting a pretty tree together in the backyard.
- Make them their favorite meal or a special treat.
- Gift your kids an experience or event by coordinating a gift treasure hunt.
- They usually like giving gifts to others as much as receiving them. Be creative in making gifts for classroom gift-giving seasons.
- Consider the gifts with a deeper significance or meaning, like a personalized journal. Also, package it thoughtfully.
- Work on projects allowing them to use their talents as gift-giving opportunities.
- Try personalized items with their names on them. For example, a simple cup or dinner plate with their name printed on it.
- Offer them cool spaces to store their mementos and new gifts, such as shadowbox shelves, open-space cabinets, or baskets.

You don't need to shower your kids with gifts. Those occasional ones will make your kids remember your love for them every time they use them. Also, gifts don't need to be store-bought ones. Other simple gift ideas include a flower on the pillowcase, a meaningful handwritten note, a piece of mail for them in the mailbox, or an "I love you" on a napkin in their lunchbox. Start charts and stickers can also help your kids feel valued. At the same time, make sure to value the gifts from your kids, whether it's a handmade card or a piece of art they made at school.

Common Pitfalls:

We need to be careful about overdoing gifts. Instead of giving them what they want, we need to gift them something appropriate for their age and can help them. Parents sometimes are tempted to shower kids with gifts rather than also use other love languages.

 # Acts of Service

These kids will feel your love when you do things for them. You may find them ask you to do something you know they're capable of. This is not because they are lazy or dependant, but because having you do these things for them will make them feel treasured by you.

Express Love to Your Kid by:

- Make a list of your kids' favorite things to do and do together periodically when they least expect it.
- Make a drink for them and bring it to them.
- Sit down to do their homework together.
- Help them organize or clean their drawers or closet.
- Give your kids some special responsibilities they like doing personally, for example, walking the dog, cooking, or watering the plants. Also, allow them to have feedbacks in the process.
- Provide your kids a surprise room makeover and consider decorating it with some pictures they like or inspiring quotes.
- When running late for the appointment, instead of just telling them to hurry up, help your kids finish what they are doing so that both of you can be ready faster.
- Create opportunities to show random kind acts to strangers together.
- Allow your kid help even when they're not so good at it.
- Pay back their acts of service through helping one of their chores secretly.
- Take time to teach. Rather than just doing everything for them, slow down

and teach your kids how to do something.
- Talk with them about how you can work with them to help your neighbors using their interests. For example, if they love animals, you can offer to help walk your neighbor's dog for free together.
- Plan simple random kind acts just for them.

Acts of service can simply be helping warm a blanket up in the dryer on a cold day, hang a wet tower up, or help them tie their shoes. This goes a long way to let your kids feel loved. While be careful and don't get in the habit of doing their chores just because they asked.

Common Pitfalls:

You don't need to jump at their every request. The thoughtful responses will do, even if they are to deny their ask. At the same time, watch out for how these exceptions to rules pile up.

The purpose of learning to speak your kids' love language is for you to have a deeper connection with your kids. Feeling love will help build their self-worth, which is critical for lifelong confidence and self-love, and this applies to all stages of development and ages.

Understanding your love language and

knowing it can be different to both your kids and your partners are powerful tools for building strong relationships and family bonds based on unconditional love, which can last for a lifetime.

Love languages are like personality traits in a person that stay with us for life. While some people's love language can change with age. Your kids' preferences may change from stage to stage. A snuggly toddler whose primary love language was physical touch may grow into a 7-year-old who prefers quality time. The kids who love to hear praises may get skeptical of your reassurance and tends to need some quality time as they grow older.

The best way to know is to stay tuned into your kids' behaviors and reactions, telling you about what type of love they need at that moment. There is no doubt that you continue to connect and reconnect as your kids grow.

2.2 How to Discipline Through Connection Applying Love Languages

Some parents may mistakenly employ the "one size fits all" parenting strategy, whether it's we've learned or read along the way or the similar techniques our parents used with us. However, the situation is we are connecting and guiding our own kids rather than ourselves. Once parents consider that every kid comes into the world with their own mind and heart, they will be able to begin exploring the more effective way to guide their kids.

If Your Kids Primary Love Language is Physical Touch:

Positive reinforcements through physical touch like hugs and high fives. Other activities involving physical touch and movement can work too, for example, having "piggy-back ride time" or playing sports together.

If Your Kids Primary Love Language is Words of Affirmation:

Consider words of encouragement, hope, and confidence. Communicate verbally or by writing. For example, "I know you are a thoughtful and nice brother and definitely don't want to hurt him. I believe you will work on using other ways to let your anger out." Communicate using specific genuine praise to their positive behaviors can go a long way.

If Your Kids Primary Love Language is Quality Time:

Develop and share activities with your kids,

such as art, reading, and games. Outings and trips to meaningful events or places are going to serve as positive long-term goals.

If Your Kids Primary Love Language is Gifts:

Create visuals or pictures to represent responsibilities and goals. Try to find concrete tangible objects to show behaviors like a friendship bracelet to help prompt the kid "treat her sister with kindness."

If Your Kids Primary Love Language is Acts of Service:

Help them enthusiastically and periodically with a responsibility or a task that they have been working on hard. For example, surprise them with a playdate even though you said there was no time or help them remember their reading homework when they forget.

Conclusion

As parents, we often think a lot about how our kids speak to us and behave. We will correct them if they need discipline, and we want to steer them away from inappropriate behaviors and make sure they use good manners. However, we may not always pay attention to what we say and the way we say it.

As anyone who worked with a child could attest, it can be challenging to communicate with kids, no matter it is a language barrier between you and the toddler, a simple misunderstanding between an adolescent and a teacher, or a battle of wills between your teenager and an authority figure, the adult-child communication can be very complicated. Research also states that the best parent-child relationships are characterized by positive interaction and communication. For a healthy parent-child relationship, parents and children not only talk when there is a conflict but talk regularly on many different topics. Researchers also believe that if adults stay in touch with kids through conversation and attention, kids may be less likely to act out or behave in the ways requiring discipline or creating conflicts.

From birth, gentle, responsive, and warm communication helps babies and children feel secure and safe in their worlds. This can build and strengthen relationships between children and their parents. As children grow and develop skills, they need security, safety, and strong relationships, so it's essential for child development to have proper communication.

Good communication involves both listening and talking in ways that can make children feel secured and valued. Inside this book, we have talked how to prepare your kids for better communication, talk to kids so they will listen to you & talk to you, solve conflicts, and use kids' love languages to communicate with them better. Using these strategies, you will not only communicate with kids better but more effectively.

Parents set a powerful example of good or poor communication. Kids' own communication skills are affected by examples they see and hear. The parents who improve their communication with kids with attention, patience, and interest set a good example.

Also, the greatest audience kids can have is an adult who is interested in them and important to them.

It is also worth remembering that kids can understand languages long before they master their speech. You could keep up with your kids' evolving language development by paying daily attention to them. If you have busy schedule, be sure to allocate some time to simply sit and listen to your kids. In brief, healthy communication with kids means respecting the kids' feelings, paying attention, and watching your voice tone.

Every kid is different, and how they receive and give love is different too. Take your time to get to know your kids' love language and express your love in the way they prefer. You will find it's not only more efficient but more rewarding.

It's time to start a conversation with your loving kids where fewer of your words get lost in translation.

Happy parenting!

From the Author

First, thank you for purchasing this book **How To Talk So Kids Will Listen & Love Languages of Kids**. We know you could have spent your time reading another book, but you have picked this book for which we are very grateful.

I hope this book added some value to your daily life. If so, it would be super nice if you could share this book with your family and friends by sharing it on *Twitter* and *Facebook*.

If you enjoyed reading this book and found some benefits from reading it, we would like to hear from you. We want you to know that your feedback and support are extremely important to us. We will appreciate it if you could take some time to **post a review** on Amazon.

You can go to **amazon.com/ryp**. Thank you!

We wish you all the best in your future success!

References

1. *6 Steps for Helping Your Child Handle Emotions. (2021, February 16). IMom. https://www.imom.com/6-steps-helping-child-handle-emotions/*

2. *Barker, E. (2018, September 9). This Is How To Raise Emotionally Intelligent Kids: 5 Secrets From Research. Barking Up The Wrong Tree. https://www.bakadesuyo.com/2018/09/emotionally-intelligent-kids/*

3. *Co., P. (2021, February 3). An Age-By-Age Guide to Helping Kids Manage Emotions.*

The Gottman Institute. https://www.gottman.com/blog/age-age-guide-helping-kids-manage-emotions/

4. *Dewar, G. (2018). Emotion coaching: Helping kids cope with negative feelings. ParentingScience. https://www.parentingscience.com/emotion-coaching.html*

5. *Gillett, T. (2020, May 17). 9 Simple Ways to Help Children Handle Their Big Feelings. Raised Good. https://raisedgood.com/9-simple-ways-to-help-children-handle-their-feelings/*

6. *Helping kids identify and express feelings. (2021, January 19). Kids Helpline. https://kidshelpline.com.au/parents/issues/helping-kids-identify-and-express-feelings*

7. *Prevent Behavior Problems by Teaching Your Child About Feelings. (2021, January 24). Verywell Family. https://www.verywellfamily.com/how-to-teach-kids-about-feelings-1095012*

8. *Wakeman, J. (2021, February 13). Helping Kids Deal With Big Emotions. Child Mind Institute. https://childmind.org/guide/parents-guide-to-problem-behavior/helping-kids-deal-with-big-emotions/*

9. *Young, K. (2020, August 17). Dealing with Big Feelings – Teaching Kids How to Self-Regulate. Hey Sigmund. https://www.heysigmund.com/how-to-self-regulate/*

10. *Glembocki, V. (2020, October 15). 5*

Empowering Ways to Get Your Kids to Listen. Parents. https://www.parents.com/parenting/better-parenting/advice/5-empowering-ways-to-get-your-kids-to-listen/

11. Hunter, W. L. (2018, February 13). *6 Pediatrician-Recommended Tips for Getting Kids to Cooperate. Parents.* https://www.parents.com/toddlers-preschoolers/development/behavioral/pediatrician-recommended-tips-for-getting-kids-to/

12. Brill, A. (2020, April 28). *35 Phrases For Encouraging Cooperation Between Child and Parent. Positive Parenting Connection.* https://www.positiveparentingconnection.net/35-phrases-for-encouraging-cooperation-between-child-and-parent/

13. *Encourage autonomy. (2018, January 11). Complex Care at Home for Children. https://complexcareathomeforchildren.com/ prepare-your-child/encourage-autonomy/*

14. *Munday, A. (2021, March 3). What is Autonomy in Early Childhood Education? HiMama Blog - Resources for Daycare Centers. https://blog.himama.com/what-is-autonomy-in-early-childhoodeducation/#:%7E:text=Autonomy%20in%20relation%20to%20early,child%20does%20in%20the%20classroom.*

15. *Garcia, N. (2020, October 9). How to Encourage Autonomy in Children. Sleeping Should Be Easy. https://sleepingshouldbeeasy.com/autonomy-in-children/*

16. Co., P. (2020, December 17). Set Kids Up For Success: How Autonomy Can Rock Their World. Parent Co. Powered by Kids2. https://www.parent.com/blogs/conversations/set-kids-success-autonomy-can-rock-world

17. Flannery, B. (2020, October 23). Causes of Conflict Between Parents and Teenagers. WeHaveKids - Family. https://wehavekids.com/parenting/Sources-of-Conflict-Between-Parents-and-Teenagers

18. Gilles, G. L. (2020). Navigating Different Types of Conflict Between Parents and Children - Child Development and Parenting: Adolescence. Mentalhelp. https://www.mentalhelp.net/blogs/navigating-different-types-of-conflict-between-parents-and-children/

19. Razo, C. L. B. J. (2018, August 21). 5 Tips to Reduce Conflict Between Parents and Children. GoodTherapy.Org Therapy Blog. https://www.goodtherapy.org/blog/5-tips-to-reduce-conflict-between-parents-children-0821185

20. Brill, A. (2017, August 27). 15 Positive Strategies for Dealing with Conflicts, Arguments & Back Talk. Positive Parenting Connection. https://www.positiveparentingconnection.net/15-positive-strategies-for-dealing-with-conflicts-arguments-back-talk/

21. Gilles, G. (n.d.). Navigating Different Types of Conflict Between Parents and Children. Gracepoint.

https://www.gracepointwellness.org/51-family-relationship-issues/article/56551-navigating-different-types-of-conflict-between-parents-and-children

22. *Author, F. S. (2020, March 20). Helping Kids Resolve Friendship Conflicts. Free Spirit Publishing Blog. https://freespiritpublishingblog.com/2017/06/08/helping-kids-resolve-friendship-conflicts/*

23. *Tired of Repeating Yourself? Here's How to Get Your Kids to Listen. (2021, April 1). Verywell Family. https://www.verywellfamily.com/kids-dont-listen-change-how-you-give-directions-1094955*

24. *Reischer, E. (2014, November 17). How to Get Your Kids to Listen the First Time.*

PsychologyToday.
https://www.psychologytoday.com/us/blog/what-great-parents-do/201411/how-get-your-kids-listen-the-first-time

25. *7 Things You Should Do When Your Child Ignores Your Directions. (2020, September 22). Verywell Family. https://www.verywellfamily.com/what-do-when-your-child-ignores-you-4105859*

26. *How Parents Can Work With a Kid Who Won't Listen. (2021, February 21). Verywell Family. https://www.verywellfamily.com/child-discipline-101-kids-wont-listen-1270213*

27. *Children's Health Team. (2021, April 5). Discipline: Top Do's and Don'ts When Your Kids Won't Listen. Health Essentials from*

Cleveland Clinic. https://health.clevelandclinic.org/discipline-top-dos-and-donts-when-your-kids-wont-listen/

28. *Spooner, R. (2016, September 23). Learning How to Love Our Kids in the Way They can Receive It. Homeschool On. https://homeschoolon.com/love-languages/*

29. *Cornwall, G. (2020, March 10). The 5 Love Languages of Children. Parents. https://www.parents.com/parenting/better-parenting/advice/love-languages-of-children/*

30. *C. (2020, September 11). What's Your Child's Love Language? The 5 Love Languages of Kids. The Pragmatic Parent.*

https://www.thepragmaticparent.com/five-love-languages-of-kids/

31. Michel, B. (n.d.). 50 Simple Ways to Speak Your Child's Love Language Everyday. FamilyFelicity.Com. https://www.familyfelicity.com/50-ways-make-your-child-feel-loved-love-language/

32. biglifejournal.com. (n.d.). How to Connect with Your Child Using Love Languages. Big Life Journal. https://biglifejournal.com/blogs/blog/connect-child-activities-love-languages

33. Pruess, A. (2020, April 19). How to Discipline Through Connection Using Your Child's Love Language. Positive Parenting Connection. https://www.positiveparentingconnection.net

/how-to-discipline-through-connection-using-your-childs-love-language/

34. *I. (2021, February 28). Love Language: The 5 Love Languages of Children. IMom. https://www.imom.com/love-language-the-5-love-languages-of-children/*

35. *Woo, M. (2018, May 28). How to Talk to Little Kids. Offspring. https://offspring.lifehacker.com/how-to-talk-to-little-kids-1826269652*

36. *Knorr, C. (2021, January 8). How to Talk to Kids About Difficult Subjects. Common Sense Media. https://www.commonsensemedia.org/blog/how-to-talk-to-kids-about-difficult-subjects*

37. *Knorr, C. (2020, October 29). Talking to Kids*

About Sexual Harassment . . . Before They Even Know About Sex. Common Sense Media. *https://www.commonsensemedia.org/blog/talking-to-kids-about-sexual-harassment-before-they-even-know-about-sex*

38. *Herrick, L. (n.d.). Guide to Telling the Children about the Divorce. Lisaherrick. https://lisaherrick.com/separation-and-divorce-work/guide-to-telling-the-children-about-the-divorce/*

39. *McCready, A. (2020, August 12). 5 Tips for Talking to Your Kids About Divorce. Positive Parenting Solutions. https://www.positiveparentingsolutions.com/parenting/talking-to-kids-about-divorce*

40. *Today's Parent. (2019, June 25). How to tell*

kids about divorce: An age-by-age guide. https://www.todaysparent.com/family/kids-and-divorce-an-age-by-age-guide/

41. Harris, N. (2018, September 6). Why It's Never Too Early to Teach Your Child Good Social Media Habits. Parents. https://www.parents.com/parenting/better-parenting/advice/why-its-never-too-early-to-teach-your-child-good-social-media/

42. Saltz, G. (2020, October 22). How to Arm Your Child Against Bullying. Child Mind Institute. https://childmind.org/article/how-to-arm-your-child-against-bullying/

43. How to talk to your children about bullying. (n.d.). UNICEF. https://www.unicef.org/end-violence/how-talk-your-children-about-bullying

44. Colino, S. L. B. (2019, August 4). How to Deal With Bullies: A Guide for. Parents. https://www.parents.com/kids/problems/bullying/bully-proof-your-child-how-to-deal-with-bullies/

45. Kadane, L. (2021, February 19). 10 proven ways to finally stop yelling at your kids. Today's Parent. https://www.todaysparent.com/family/discipline/proven-ways-to-finally-stop-yelling-at-your-kids/

46. Gagne, C. (2020, September 10). Age-by-age guide to getting your kid to talk to you. Today's Parent. https://www.todaysparent.com/family/age-by-age-guide-to-getting-your-kid-to-talk

Made in the USA
Columbia, SC
04 February 2022